Famous Christians

Famous Christians

IN BAHÁ'Í HISTORY

§

Third in the 'Christian Believers'
Series. Books especially
written for Christians exploring the Bahá'í Faith

§

MISSIONARIES, PHYSICIANS, DIPLOMATS, ARMY CAPTAINS, GENERALS, AN INTELLIGENCE OFFICER, KINGS, QUEENS, ARTISTS, AUTHORS, MUSICIANS, DANCERS, BIBLE SCHOLARS, POLITICIANS, SCIENTISTS, AND A HOST OF ORDINARY PEOPLE, ALL CHRISTIANS, PLAYED IMPORTANT ROLES IN THE BAHÁ'Í STORY, INCLUDING ONE CHRISTIAN WHO GAVE HIS LIFE TO SAVE THE LIFE OF BAHÁ'U'LLÁH.

Thom Thompson
AUTHOR OF: *QUESTIONS FROM CHRISTIANS:
ABOUT BAHÁ'U'LLÁH AND THE BAHÁ'Í FAITH*

§

© 2017 Thom Thompson
All rights reserved.

ISBN-13: 9781516845682
ISBN-10: 1516845684

Table of Contents

Dedication · vii
Introduction · ix

Chapter 1 A Brief History of the Bahá'í Faith · · · · · · · · · · · 1
Chapter 2 Bahá'u'lláh's Spiritual and Social Teachings; What they could Mean for Christians and the World · 30
Chapter 3 Why this book was Written · · · · · · · · · · · · · · · 67
Chapter 4 Why call these Christians 'Famous'? · · · · · · · · · 79
Chapter 5 A Canon of the Church, A Biblical Scholar, a Queen…and a King (all of whom became Bahá'ís.) · 92
Chapter 6 More Kings, and another Queen, and a President of the United States · · · · · · · · · · · · 107
Chapter 7 Still more Kings, and a Pope! And a Governor · 126
Chapter 8 A Jazz Musician and a Famous African-American Scholar, both of whom became Bahá'ís. And a Botanist, Revered Arabic Scholar, a Russian Novelist, Middle-Eastern Scholar, and Two Presidents of Czechoslovakia. And, let's throw in an a Presidential Candidate and an Inventor · · · · · · 145

Chapter 9   Some Nameless but nevertheless Famous
                      Christians 167
Chapter 10 Two Army Captains, two Generals, some
                      Monks and a Watchmaker. Plus, more on
                      the first Christian to become a Bahá'í 191
Chapter 11 The Christian who saved the life of
                      Bahá'u'lláh and the Christian who gave
                      his life so that Bahá'u'lláh might live Plus:
                      Bahá'u'lláh wrote a letter to you! 212
Chapter 12 'Letter to the Christians.' A letter that
                      Bahá'u'lláh wrote to all Christians and
                      therefore: To you 219

                      Bibliography 237

Dedication

This book describing the roles played by many Christians in the history and development of the Bahá'í Faith is lovingly dedicated to my professors at Vanderbilt University School of Divinity, among them Bard Thompson and Roger Shinn, as well as Nels F. S. Ferré and, of special note, Kendrick Grobel and George Noel Mayhew. All of them were inspiring as well as informative. I feel a heavy debt of gratitude to God for their presence in my life.

Introduction

THIS BOOK IS THE THIRD in a series called: 'The Christian Believer Series.' The first in the series, published in 2001 was *Questions from Christians: About Bahá'u'lláh and the Bahá'í Faith.* This was my best attempt to answer any and all questions that Christians might have when they first learn of Bahá'u'lláh and the Bahá'í Faith. In some ways, the book was written in response to my *own* questions that occurred to me when first hearing of the coming of Bahá'u'lláh and the establishment of the Bahá'í Faith.

Next came *Every Good Thing: A Personal Selection of Bahá'í Scripture Chosen Especially for Christian Believers.* This current book, *Famous Christians: In Bahá'í History* is again designed for believers in Christ, connecting their interest in the Bahá'í Faith to the many Christians who played a role in Bahá'í history.

What a surprise it was for me as an author of Bahá'í books and a person deeply interested in Bahá'í history, to find that the history of the unfolding of the Bahá'í Faith included a throng of Christian believers who show up when looking at the history of that Faith. Some of the roles played by Christian believers are marginal, but as I will explain later, there is a way to view them as important historically. Others are pivotal and significant, including one instance, for example, where an entire community of Bahá'í believers was starving and near death and the only persons who came to their aid were Christians. Some roles played by Christians were anything but marginal, including one person who acted to save Bahá'u'lláh's life and most surprising of all, a Christian who sacrificed his life so that Bahá'u'lláh could live.

The rationale for why this book is being written will be given in the first chapter, but for now let me say that this book is a paean of praise for these Christian believers as well as a recognition of the roles they played in the drama of Bahá'í History.

There are about fifty or more Christians in this account, but many more could have been included. These fifty, though, are a personal selection and the ones I found most intriguing and memorable. I hope and believe you will enjoy learning about them and assessing their lives, actions and, in some few instances, their contribution to the historical unfolding of the Faith of Bahá'u'lláh.

One important note: Every 'famous Christian' referenced in this book is an actual historical figure. Within or after each section describing an individual, you will see documentation in a footnote. When Jesus and Bahá'u'lláh are quoted (or others), the source will be referenced in parenthesis in the text. You can then refer to the bibliography for complete information as to source.

So have at it. Believe me, I did not expect to find these Christians saying what they said and doing what they did in Bahá'í history. I hope you enjoy their story.

§

But before we begin, a word about the organization of this book. I am aware that some people who pick up this book will already know quite a bit about the Bahá'í Faith and the teachings of Bahá'u'lláh. If you are that kind of reader, please feel free to skip the first two chapters: Chapter One: 'A Brief History of the Bahá'í Faith' and Chapter Two: 'The Teachings of Bahá'u'lláh: What they could mean for the Christian and for the world.'

However, if you are learning about the Bahá'í Faith and about Bahá'u'lláh for the first time or if you feel the need for more information, you may want to read chapters one and two to learn more about the Revelation of God brought by Bahá'u'lláh and His teachings which are the foundation of the Bahá'í Faith.

CHAPTER 1

A Brief History of the Bahá'í Faith

How it all Began: the Coming of Bahá'u'lláh And The Beginning Of The Bahá'í Faith

[NOTE: Chapters one and two are excerpted from *Questions from Christians: About Bahá'u'lláh and the Bahá'í Faith*.]

QUESTION: It may sound strange to you but I've never heard of the Bahá'í Faith and many persons I know have never heard about it, so I need you to give me information about where, when and how the Bahá'í Faith began.

RESPONSE: Actually, in Christian terms, it's pretty fascinating, as you will see. During the mid-1800's, the time of your great, or great, great grandparents, Christians were strong in their expectation of the imminent return of Jesus, which they thought would be immediate. They were fervently awaiting Him and they thought it would happen any day. One Christian minister, William Miller, even picked the year, using biblical prophecy, as 1843 or early 1844. Christians in the United States and around

1

the world heard and believed this prediction and eagerly awaited Christ's Return.

When the promised return did not occur within Miller's time-frame, he looked again at his calculations and discovered that he had, he said, made a mistake about the "time of the end" and now pronounced that the Return of Jesus would happen on October 22, 1844, one year later than earlier predicted. His followers, the Millerites, from whom several modern-day churches derive, were disappointed when the promised return still did not occur. The groups that developed later partly as a result of the ferment caused by the Millerites (the 'Bible Student Movement,' the Jehovah's Witnesses and the Seventh Day Adventists, among others) have often referred to this experience as "The Great Disappointment." Not only these smaller groups, but Methodists, Presbyterians, Baptists and even Episcopalians were excited about the imminent return of Christ.

However, from the Bahá'í perspective, Christ's Return *did* occur, but in a different way than was expected by Rev. Miller, his followers, and millions of Christians around the world, who were caught up in a 'millennial fervor.' It was not just the 'Millerites' who believed this. It was widely believed by millions of people of Christian background around the world, of all classes. Speeches were made in the United States Congress about it.

William Miller

QUESTION: You are saying Christ's Return *did* occur?

RESPONSE: Bahá'ís believe that it did occur, that when Bahá'u'lláh appeared He was the Return of Christ to the world. If that is a shocking statement, I can relate very well to how you might feel, since I experienced a whole range of feelings when I first heard this claim, from disgust, to anger, to curiosity and, finally, to the point of wanting to know more.

History is often ironic, isn't it? Especially in this case, since May 23, 1844 is the date on which the Bahá'í Faith begins, with a fresh outpouring of God's Grace and an event that signaled, Bahá'ís believe, the Return of Christ. Bahá'ís believe Rev. Miller was right, somehow spiritually attuned and should not have felt 'disappointed'. And, though it is not well-known to most Christians, part of the Muslim world also expected an announcement of a prophetic messenger around the same date. In fact, all the other major faiths, even the religions of the Native Americans and other indigenous peoples pointed to this general time in history as the time of fulfillment of prophecy.

QUESTION: So Bahá'u'lláh appeared in 1844?

RESPONSE: No, because just as was the case with Jesus, Who was preceded by John the Baptist announcing His coming, Bahá'u'lláh also had a forerunner, a young merchant of Shiraz, Persia (modern day Iran) who proclaimed to the world that the 'Promise of All Ages' was about to appear. The young merchant, a Manifestation of God in His own right, Bahá'ís believe, is known by His title: The Báb (which means 'Gate'). The symbolism was clear, namely, that 'the Báb' was the 'Gate' through which the long awaited Promised One of all Religions would walk. The Báb called this Promised One ***"Him Whom God shall make manifest"*** (The Báb: *Selections from the Báb*, 7)

(The Báb's name is pronounced with an 'ah' sound, rather than with a short 'a', almost as if saying 'bob.')

Though it is not included in this book, there is a chapter in my previous book - *Questions from Christians* - about 'Progressive Revelation,' a new way of looking at history and trying to understand it in a radically new way. When you understand what Bahá'ís mean by 'Progressive Revelation,' I hope you will begin to see why they are so excited about the prospect of human unity expressed by an oft-used Bahá'í phrase: 'One God, One Planet, One People.'

We spoke of the Báb, Bahá'u'lláh's predecessor a moment ago. When the Báb set forth His mission and began His ministry, the whole of Persia (modern Iran) was set into an uproar, for many people responded to His message and followed His new Faith. His central message was the imminent coming of the Promised One of all Ages. His followers began to eagerly await the appearance of **"Him Whom God shall make manifest"** which was soon to happen.

The Báb said that this Promised One would appear for the sake of the whole world, to unite the world's peoples, to bring together the races, religions and cultures of that world and to bring about the Golden Age of fulfillment of the prophecies of all religions.

In an historical moment reminding us of John the Baptist and Jesus, there was a follower of the Báb named Mirzá Husayn Ali (known later as Bahá'u'lláh). As mentioned earlier, the birth name of Jesus was Jesus of Nazareth while His title later on was 'Christ', meaning 'The Anointed One.' In this same way, Bahá'u'lláh had both a birth name and a title - Bahá'u'lláh - which means 'The Glory of God'. Just as Jesus began His ministry as a follower of John the Baptist (even going to John to be baptized), Bahá'u'lláh began His ministry as a follower of the Báb.

But going back to the Báb, His religion grew so quickly that the state and religious leaders were alarmed. Remember Annas and Caiaphas (religious leaders in the time of Jesus) and Herod (leader of the state) and Pilate (Roman Prefect) who were alarmed at how the people were responding to Jesus? For that matter, these same religious leaders and state leaders were greatly alarmed at the following of John the Baptist.

The same thing happened to the Báb as happened to both John the Baptist and Jesus. The clergy and the state had the Báb executed on

July 9, 1850. An account of the apparently miraculous martyrdom of the Báb can be found in the *Encyclopedia Britannica*, but let me whet your interest by telling you that even though seven hundred fifty rifles were used to attempt to execute the Báb, He was unscathed and nowhere to be found after the first fusillade of rifle fire and the clearing of the tremendous cloud of smoke.

Prison guards eventually found Him back in His cell, where He told them that they could now carry out their intention, as His mission was finished. And, they now carried out His execution in the same fashion. Look up this entire story (in *The Dawnbreakers*, a history written by one of Bahá'u'lláh's disciples) or have a Bahá'í friend tell it to you in detail because it is a fascinating historical moment.

Sam Khan, a Captain in the Army, was a Christian who was reluctant to carry out the execution. He feared the wrath of God, he told his men, if he put to death a holy man. He talked with the Báb, saying: "I profess the Christian Faith and entertain no ill will toward you. If your cause be the Cause of Truth, enable me to free myself from the obligation to shed your blood." The Báb replied: "Follow your instructions, and if your intention be sincere, the Almighty is surely able to relieve you of your perplexity." (Cedarquist, *The Story of Bahá'u'lláh*, 2005, 82)

Perplexity it was, for on the one hand, he had an order from the highest level of government; on the other hand, he did not want to do an unjust act against someone Who was a descendant of the Prophet Mohammed and a person who said He brought a new message from God. Based on what the Báb had said, Sam Khan proceeded with the execution. The short version is this: After seven-hundred fifty rifles had been discharged, the Báb was nowhere to be found.

Moments later, the Báb was discovered back in His prison room, telling the executioners they could now proceed with their plan, as He had now finished His work on earth. Sam Khan promptly refused to go through with the final execution and another regiment was brought in who carried out the deed.

I will include here the last words that the Báb spoke before seven hundred fifty bullets tore through His body. The words were spoken to 10,000 people who had gathered in a barracks square and on the rooftops to witness His execution. A young man had begged the Báb to be allowed to die with Him. The Báb spoke to those assembled before Him and said:

"O wayward generation!" were the last words of the Báb to the gazing multitude, as the regiment prepared to fire its volley *"Had you believed in Me every one of you would have followed the example of this youth, who stood in rank above most of you, and would have willingly sacrificed himself in My path. The day will come when you will have recognized Me; that day I shall have ceased to be with you."* Shoghi Effendi. *God Passes By*, 1944, 53)

QUESTION: What happened then? And where does Bahá'u'lláh come into the picture?

RESPONSE: As I began to tell you earlier, Bahá'u'lláh was a follower of the Báb, just as Jesus at one point was a follower of John the Baptist. The Báb was martyred in 1850. Persia was still in chaos, with the government and clergy intent upon exterminating the community of the followers of the Báb over the years.

They martyred 20,000 or more people who chose to die rather than give up their Faith. Most of them were offered life if they would utter one word of denial but few chose that path. The Báb's followers were true to His central message that God would very soon make Himself known in a way awaited by the entire world. They were eagerly awaiting the appearance of ***"Him Whom God shall make manifest."***

In 1853, three years after the martyrdom of the Báb, Bahá'u'lláh had been cast into a prison dungeon called 'The Black Pit,' along with other followers of the Báb. It was in this dark, oppressive dungeon that Bahá'u'lláh received God's Revelation, fully realizing for the first time that He was ***"Him Whom God shall make manifest"*** and the One sent by God, the 'Promised One of All Ages.'

When Jesus was baptized, a dove, symbolizing the Holy Spirit, hovered above His head and there was, the New Testament tells us, a voice that said: ***"You are My beloved Son; in You I am well pleased."*** (Luke 3:22)

Bahá'u'lláh's experience in the dungeon bears a striking similarity to the story of the Holy Spirit descending upon Jesus in the form of a dove. This is what happened: There appeared before Bahá'u'lláh, suspended in the air above His head, that same Holy Spirit, symbolized by a beautiful maiden, who pointed at His head and said: ***"Verily, We shall render Thee victorious by Thyself and by Thy pen. Grieve Thou not for that which hath befallen Thee, neither be***

Thou afraid, for Thou art in safety. Ere long will God raise up the treasures of the earth - men who will aid Thee through Thyself and through Thy Name, wherewith God hath revived the hearts of such as have recognized Him." (Bahá'u'lláh: *God Passes By*, 1944, 101)

We are allowed a 'rare' glimpse at what happens when a 'Manifestation' of God begins to realize that God will be speaking and acting through Him as Bahá'u'lláh shares with us what happened next. He is still in the dungeon:

"During the days I lay in the prison of Tihran [the dungeon was in the capital city of Iran, now spelled as Teheran]*...though the galling weight of the chains and the stench-filled air allowed Me but little sleep, still in those infrequent moments of slumber I felt as if something flowed from the crown of My head over My breast, even as a mighty torrent that precipitateth itself upon the earth from the summit of a lofty mountain. Every limb of My body would, as a result, be set afire. At such moments My tongue recited what no man could bear to hear."*

(Shoghi Effendi: *God Passes By*, 1944, 101)

Later in His ministry, Bahá'u'lláh referred to a time when He was well aware of the Divine Presence in His life and His Ministry. He said: *"And whenever I chose to hold my peace and be still, lo, the voice of the Holy Ghost, standing on my right hand, aroused me, and the Supreme Spirit appeared before my face, and Gabriel overshadowed me, and the Spirit of Glory stirred within my bosom, bidding me arise and break my silence."* (Bahá'u'lláh, *Gleanings From the Writings of Bahá'u'lláh*, 1939, 103)

The Shrine of the Báb on the crest of Mount Carmel, Haifa, Israel

When Bahá'u'lláh was released, He was banished from Persia to Baghdad, Iraq, then to Constantinople (now Istanbul), then to Adrianople (now Edirne), and finally, to a prison city - 'Akká- in Syria (now Israel). The clergy of Iran and the Sultan of the Ottoman Empire were attempting to remove Bahá'u'lláh far from Persia so that His influence on His followers would wane. They did not realize that the 'Divine Light' cannot be extinguished, not in a dungeon or in a faraway prison city. Many writers and scholars of the Bahá'í Faith have noted that Bahá'u'lláh's successive banishment and imprisonment seemed to be in fulfillment of Biblical prophecy.

His final banishment was to the city of 'Akká, in the vicinity of Mt. Carmel, the 'Mountain of the Lord' in the Old Testament. This is where the Bahá'í World Center now exists and it is also where the remains of the Báb lie in a beautiful shrine. The city of Haifa, Israel, lies at the foot of the 'Mountain of the Lord' and its citizens look up to the Bahá'í Shrines in the bosom of that mountain. In the early part of the Twenty-First Century, more than one non-Bahá'í writer has referred to the gardens and terraces of the Shrine of the Báb as one of the 'Wonders of the modern world.

On the eve of His banishment from Baghdad (April, 1863), Bahá'u'lláh spent several days in a garden named Ridvan (the name in Arabic means 'Paradise'). He had waited a full ten years to announce His Mission to the world, which He now did, while camped in that Garden. Over the next thirty years, though He was subject to continuous banishment, imprisonment or house arrest, He continued to pour forth the stream of God's new Revelation. Neither torture, nor isolation, nor condemnation by the authorities could keep Him from unfolding God's Will for humanity.

QUESTION: Let me interrupt you for a moment! It sounds as if Bahá'u'lláh was a criminal. The state punished Him, put Him in prison, banished Him and kept Him under house arrest. Was He a criminal? If so, why are you talking about Him in this reverential way?

RESPONSE: Well, I can understand your confusion. Do we consider Christ to be a criminal? Of course not! We don't think that way about Christ at all, do we? But we have to remember that Jesus was 'legally' executed as a criminal on several criminal charges put forth by religious and state leaders. He was condemned by the top religious leaders and the leaders of the state, Caiaphas, Annas, Pilate and Herod.

So I guess it's a point of view: State and religious leaders thought Christ was a criminal, and the Sultan of the Ottoman Empire thought Bahá'u'lláh was a criminal, but now that time has gone by, we realize that those religious and temporal leaders were not only short-sighted, but wrong. Pilate missed recognizing the **'Son of God'** - Jesus. Likewise, Sultan Abdu'l-'Azíz, missed recognizing the **'Father'** - Bahá'u'lláh. (Bahá'u'lláh: *God Passes By*, 1944, 17)

Bahá'u'lláh suffered continued banishment and finally imprisonment over the next thirty years (1863-1892); He steadily revealed what God had commissioned Him to give to humanity. A mighty torrent of scripture poured forth, which exists in His handwriting or under His seal in their original form. There are more than fifteen- thousand documents, papers and letters and numerous book-length writings.[1]

Bahá'u'lláh suffered all His life, saying, on one occasion: **"I have been, most of the days of My life...sitting under a sword hanging on a thread."** (Bahá'u'lláh: *Epistle to the Son of the Wolf*, p. 94). However, Bahá'u'lláh said His sufferings had a purpose: **"I have accepted to be tried by manifold adversities for no purpose except to regenerate all**

---

1 Bahá'u'lláh stated that he had brought forth the equivalent of one-hundred volumes in His Revelation. See Robert Stockman here: bahai-library.com/number_tablets_Bahá'u'lláh, for detail on the figure of 15,000 documents from Bahá'u'llah's pen. Also, the author has spoken at length with a paper conservator who worked at the Bahá'í World Center for a number of years, who stated she and others feel that there is an unknown larger number of these documents from the Pen of Bahá'u'lláh which are sought to be authenticated, perhaps as many as 20,000 for the grand total. There is an on-going search for documents. However, we can be reasonably sure that the central documents in Bahá'u'lláh's Revelation have already been presented in the several books from Bahá'u'lláh's Pen, in the '*Gleanings*' and other books and letters produced by the Guardian, Shoghi Effendi and more recently, the Universal House of Justice.

that are in Thy heaven and on Thy earth." Bahá'u'lláh, *Prayers and Meditations*, 1954, 198) And, He said that He *"hath consented to be bound with chains that mankind may be released from its bondage, and hath accepted to be made a prisoner within this most mighty Stronghold that the whole world may attain unto true liberty. He hath drained to its dregs the cup of sorrow, that all the peoples of the earth may attain unto abiding joy, and be filled with gladness."* (Bahá'u'lláh: *Gleanings*, 1939, 99)

QUESTION: Bahá'u'lláh may have gone to prison, but Jesus was sacrificed upon the cross for the sins of the world. God sacrificed His own Son! Don't you appreciate the significance of that?

RESPONSE: This sacrifice was amazing and significant. Bahá'u'lláh speaks of it often. But regarding being sent to prison, which He accepted as God's Will, Bahá'u'lláh spoke of Himself as the One *"Whom Thou hast sacrificed that all the dwellers of Thine earth and heaven may be born anew, and Whom Thou hast cast into prison that mankind may, as a token of Thy bounty and of Thy sovereign might, be released from the bondage of evil passions and corrupt desires."* (Bahá'u'lláh: *Prayers and Meditations*, 1938, 44)

You will hear, as we continue our conversation, that Bahá'u'lláh teaches that God has sacrificed over and over again in the sending of Manifestations of Himself to humanity. Each of them has suffered and sacrificed in a significant way. Each time, this sacrifice, this suffering, has been for the sins of the world and the salvation of all.

Also, regarding the purpose of His imprisonment, Bahá'u'lláh said: *"My body hath endured imprisonment that ye may be released from the bondage of self."* (Taherzadeh: *Tablets of Bahá'u'lláh*, 1978, 12) Christians believe that Christ's suffering was for the salvation of all the individuals in the world. Bahá'ís believe the same thing about Christ. The difference is that Bahá'u'lláh taught that His own suffering and the suffering of all the Manifestations of God was for the world's salvation and regeneration, as well as for salvation for individuals. More on this later in Chapter Nine: 'Similarities and Differences between the Christian and Bahá'í Faiths.' (Note: This chapter referred to here is not in this book but can be found in my earlier book, *Questions from Christians*.)

In 1892, Bahá'u'lláh's Spirit ascended. He left a Will and Testament, naming His Son, 'Abdu'l-Bahá (His name means 'Servant of Bahá'u'lláh') to lead the community of Bahá'ís and, more importantly, to be what He called the **"Center of my Covenant"** with the Bahá'ís and with all humankind. Bahá'u'lláh said that God has always set forth a **"Covenant"** with mankind and that whenever a new Manifestation of God appears in our human history, this 'Covenant' is being renewed.

Likewise, each Manifestation makes a 'Covenant' with His followers. Bahá'u'lláh's 'Covenant' with mankind involved telling His followers to turn toward 'Abdu'l-Bahá as the only one who was authorized to interpret the meaning of His revelation. In this way, unity, so important not only to the Bahá'ís but to the world, could be maintained. As a result, 'Abdu'l-Bahá is central in the Bahá'í Faith, and His writings and prayers are very dear to the Bahá'ís and considered part of our Scripture. I will conclude this chapter with several prayers from 'Abdu'l-Bahá.

Bahá'u'lláh asked that the Bahá'ís embrace and vigorously pursue the task of healing and uniting the world. He indicated this would prove impossible *"unless the peoples of the world unite in pursuit of one common aim and embrace one universal faith."* (Bahá'u'lláh, *Tablets of Bahá'u'lláh*, 1978, 69) He also charged the Bahá'ís with the task of electing a *"House of Justice"* (a governing body) in every community in the world where there are nine or more Bahá'ís. These 'Houses of Justice' are called 'Local Spiritual Assemblies' at this time in Bahá'í history. (There are more than ten thousand of them around the world.)

Finally, He asked that when the Faith had spread throughout the world (which was finally accomplished in the 1950's) that the worldwide Bahá'í Community should elect a 'Universal House of Justice.' This institution, the direct creation of Bahá'u'lláh and drawn from all over the world, was elected for the first time in 1963. Bahá'u'lláh called this Universal House of Justice (and all of the Local and Spiritual Assemblies around the world) *"the Trustees of the All-Merciful"* and *"the Trustees of God among His servants and the daysprings of authority in His countries."* (Bahá'u'lláh, *Tablets of Bahá'u'lláh*, 1978, 26) Therefore, Bahá'ís see these institutions as divinely ordained, having the task of administering all the affairs of the worldwide Bahá'í Community and ultimately contributing to the building of a united world.

Bahá'u'lláh left a great legacy of scripture to guide the Bahá'ís but said that for anything not covered in His Revelation, the Bahá'ís were to turn to this Universal House of Justice. They would decide based upon what Bahá'u'lláh called *"the needs and requirements of the time."* He gave them the task of being *"a shelter for the poor and needy"* and charged them to act in the *"protection and safeguarding"* of humankind. (Bahá'u'lláh, *Tablets of Bahá'u'lláh*, 27, 28, 69)

Most important of all, Bahá'u'lláh assured that this institution would have Divine Guidance, saying: *"God will verily inspire them* [i.e., the Universal House of Justice] *with whatsoever He willeth."* He asked them to *"take counsel together regarding those things which have not outwardly been revealed in the Book"* [2] telling them once again that they would be the *"recipients of divine inspiration from the unseen Kingdom"*. (Bahá'u'lláh, *Tablets of Bahá'u'lláh*, 1978, 68, 27)

Because of His appointment of His son 'Abdu'l-Bahá as the sole interpreter of His Revelation and because of the guidance of God that He bestowed on the Universal House of Justice, the Bahá'í Faith has not fallen victim to disunity, which very often occurs quickly after the founder of a religion has died, as sadly happened in both Christianity and Islam.

QUESTION: You said a moment ago that the Bahá'í Faith had spread over the entire planet. I doubt that. Wouldn't I have heard about it if it were so widespread?

RESPONSE: The Bahá'í Faith is not trying to be silent or secret. Every Bahá'í would like to 'shout from the rooftops' but yes, somehow this interesting development has occurred right now in the Twentieth Century. I guess most of humanity has been looking the

---

2 Bahá'u'lláh states here 'the Book,' but this does not refer alone to his *Kitáb-i-Aqdas* (Most Holy Book), but to His entire Revelation.

other way, as they were when Christ came. The world at large took almost no note of the Christian Faith for several hundred years. When they did take note, it was to see Christianity as a 'dangerous cult' with atheistic tendencies. (Christians refused to believe in or to sacrifice to the Roman 'gods,' so to Roman citizens, they were atheists, as strange as that sounds; one reader of this book, Rev. Barbara Berry-Bailey comments that another reason they were considered atheists was that they had an 'invisible' God, with no idols or statues to worship.)

If you would like a reference on the spread of the Bahá'í Faith, consult the Encyclopedia Britannica, which in 1996 declared the Bahá'í Faith to be the world's most widespread religion, second only to Christianity. Let me tease you; maybe you were looking the other way at wars, cold wars, atomic explosions, revolutions, terrorism, and the like, while ***"the Father"*** - Bahá'u'lláh - put in His appearance. Two thousand years ago, many Romans were definitely 'looking the other way' and missed the appearance of ***"The Son of God."***

The Bahá'ís have received a definite charge from Bahá'u'lláh, a mission to unite the world. You have already told me that this mission sounds grandiose, but I don't have a choice about whether or not to tell you about it because that is precisely what Bahá'u'lláh asked Bahá'ís to do. We believe humanity's accomplishment of this mission of unity and peace is God's Will for today's world and today's people. Bahá'ís have already been hard at work in the Twentieth Century, while the people of the world were 'looking the other way,' to spread the Faith of Bahá'u'lláh and to broadcast His teachings. We believe those teachings will have a transforming effect on a world so much in need.

So, while the world seemed to be 'coming apart' in the Twentieth Century, as destruction and devastation and planetary breakdown seemed to be the order of the day, there was another process going on - a process of a new and different world slowly, surely being built, a new world that mankind has been long awaiting, a world of peace, unity and fulfillment. This is the way Bahá'u'lláh put it:

"O friends! It behoveth you to refresh and revive your souls through the gracious favors which in this Divine, this soul-stirring Springtime are being showered upon you. The Day Star of His great glory hath shed its radiance upon you, and the clouds of His limitless grace have overshadowed you. How high the reward of him that hath not deprived himself of so great a bounty, nor failed to recognize the beauty of his Best-Beloved in this, His new attire." (Bahá'u'lláh, *Gleanings*, 1939, 94)

"Say: O men! This is a matchless Day. Matchless must, likewise, be the tongue that celebrateth the praise of the Desire of all nations, and matchless the deed that aspireth to be acceptable in His sight. The whole human race hath longed for this Day, that perchance it may fulfill that which well beseemeth its station, and is worthy of its destiny. Blessed is the man whom the affairs of the world have failed to deter from recognizing Him Who is the Lord of all things." (ibid, 38)

And: *"This is the Day whereon the Ocean of God's mercy hath been manifested unto men, the Day in which the Day Star of His loving-kindness hath shed its radiance upon them, the Day in which the clouds of His bountiful favor have overshadowed the whole of mankind. Now is the time to cheer and refresh the down-cast through the invigorating breeze of love and fellowship, and the living waters of friendliness and charity."* (ibid, 7)

"Take heed lest anything deter thee from extolling the greatness of this Day - the Day whereon the Finger of majesty and power hath opened the seal of the Wine of Reunion, and called all who are in the heavens and all who are on the earth. Preferrest thou to tarry when the breeze announcing the Day of God hath already breathed over thee, or art thou of them that are shut out as by a veil from Him?" (ibid, 28)

Also: *"Say: He Who is the Unconditioned is come, in the clouds of light, that He may quicken all created things with the breezes of His Name, the Most Merciful, and unify the world, and gather all men around this Table which hath been sent down from heaven."* (Bahá'u'lláh: *Epistle to the Son of the Wolf*, 1979, 46) *"Darkness hath been chased away by the dawning light of the mercy of thy Lord, the Source of all light. The breeze of the All-Merciful hath wafted, and the souls have been quickened in the tombs of their bodies."* (Bahá'u'lláh, *Tablets of Bahá'u'lláh*, 1978, 118)

Finally: *"The hands of bounty have borne round the cup of everlasting life. Approach, and quaff your fill..."* Bahá'u'lláh, *Gleanings*, 1939, 32)

So, charged by Bahá'u'lláh, Bahá'ís labored mightily to take the healing message of the Faith into every corner of the Earth. As I told you, this was accomplished by 1963, so that the Universal House of Justice could be elected. Bahá'ís are still concentrating on bringing this message to every human being on the planet. While this 'outreach' is occurring, the Bahá'ís are also constructing a World Center in Haifa, Israel, as I mentioned earlier.[3]

This nerve center in the Holy Land (now 'holy' to four Faiths - Judaism, Christianity, Islam and the Bahá'í Faith[4]) is serving to coordinate and energize the spread of the message of the coming of Bahá'u'lláh and His teachings. The goal of this world center and of the Bahá'ís over the entire world is none other than the unification of the human race, under one God. Daunting? Impossible? Consider this: Wouldn't it have been well-nigh impossible to have told the early Christians that they wouldn't be able to fulfill the commandment of Christ to **"Go into all the world, and preach the gospel to every creature"**? (Mark 16:15) Bahá'ís, like those early Christians, are confident that they can, with divine assistance, take this message to every person in the world.

---

3 During the first decade of the 21st century, the architectural 'Arc' of buildings was all but finished, save for the building of an International Library. In that decade, the magnificent 'terraces' below and above the Shrine of the Bab were finished. The building of these eighteen terraces was, at that time, the largest building project in Israel and top Israeli leaders visited them. Also in this time period, the building of the International Teaching Center and, as well, the Center for the Study of the Texts.

4 You know that both David and Christ were descended from Abraham's first wife, Sarah. You probably also know that Muhammad was descended from the second wife, Hagar. What is less known is that both Zoroaster and Bahá'u'lláh were descended from the third wife, Keturah (cf. Gen. 25:1). This all makes God's Promise to Abraham convincingly real: *"I will make your descendants as numerous as the stars in the sky and will give them all these lands, and through your offspring all nations on earth will be blessed..."* (cf. Gen. 26:4). To hear the whole story, read: Frances Worthington. *Abraham: One God, Three Wives, Five Religions* . (Wilmette, IL: Bahá'í Publishing Trust, 2011).

QUESTION: To me, you seem a little vague when you talk about a 'healing, uniting message.' Just how do the Bahá'ís even hope to make an impact on a world like the one we have now, so disunited, violent, and angry?

RESPONSE: Two ways. First, wherever there are Bahá'ís, there is a community of men and women, young adults, youth and children, who live their lives by a renewed power of the Holy Spirit instilled in them by Bahá'u'lláh and by a set of teachings given by Bahá'u'lláh, teachings that are remarkable by any standard. These are teachings that affect individual behavior, then go on to affect the way a community of people act and react toward each other and to the world at large. You can learn more about the Bahá'í teachings in the next chapter, but for the moment, imagine the following:

Imagine that you are driving through the mid-west of the United States or through Spain or through sub-Saharan Africa or in South America or through Indonesia. Imagine yourself to be *anywhere* on the planet and the person riding with you says: "Did you know that an unusual group of people live in the town (or village) just ahead?" You reply: "Why are they so different?"

Your friend says: "Listen to this. The people in this village or town all believe in the equality of men and women, *every last one of them.* They *all* are trying very hard to eradicate all forms of prejudice from their individual and community lives. They *all* believe not only in Jesus, but also in Buddha, Muhammad, Moses, Zoroaster and all the manifestations of God that have appeared in human history. They *all* believe in the oneness of religion, the oneness of God, the oneness of the human race. Many of them intermarry between the so-called 'races' and even promote intermarriage."

You probably would say: "That couldn't be true, could it?" Your friend continues that everyone in this small village considers themselves 'world citizens' and that they support the establishment of a universal language. Then, finally, because you don't believe him at all, your friend tells you that the village ahead is a Bahá'í village and that, in fact, wherever Bahá'ís live on the planet, in whatever country, they are conducting their lives by these values and beliefs given them by Bahá'u'lláh, who said: *"I can utter no word, O my God, unless I be permitted by Thee, and can move in no direction until I obtain Thy sanction. It is Thou, O my God, Who hast called me into being through the power of Thy might, and hast endued me with Thy grace to manifest Thy Cause."* (Bahá'u'lláh, *Prayers and Meditations*, 1938, 208)

Today, there is a worldwide network of Bahá'ís, all united in the set of objectives mentioned above, all of them focused on a goal of the recognition and the creation of human unity.

QUESTION: You said there was a second way, besides your teachings and your community life that Bahá'ís would use to make a practical impact upon the world. You certainly do know that nice and beautiful teachings alone won't really do much. What about human nature, and what about 'sin'?

RESPONSE: You couldn't be more right about that last point. If all that the Bahá'í Faith had to offer were a new set of teachings, it wouldn't be enough, no matter how beautiful or compelling. In fact, the teachings are secondary to the appearance of Bahá'u'lláh, who brings the Divine energy needed for these tasks that the teachings propose and, more importantly, Bahá'u'lláh brings salvation not just for individuals, but also for a dying, failing world.

One of the proofs of Jesus Christ, when He appeared the first time, was that those who followed Him began to lead changed, transformed lives, full of new and more positive values and beliefs, people who were energized with a new set of goals and who led individual and community lives that expressed a new ethic, a new culture and, in essence, a new world.

This is exactly what is happening when a person follows Bahá'u'lláh. Bahá'u'lláh tells us He is the Return of Christ to the world as well as the appearance of ***"The Father"*** of all mankind. This follower, this person is transformed, saved, brought into a new life, infused with new values and ideas and charged with a mission to enact, with others, the reality of a united humanity. The old saying that 'the proof of the pudding is in the eating' probably applies here. While the proof of the Baha'i Faith is not only to be seen in the lives and communities of the Baha'is, you can take a look at the Bahá'í communities and witness what is going on. If Baha'is are not leading transformed lives, if their communities are not vibrant examples of a unifying force for humanity, then your question of who Bahá'u'lláh is gets really easy. In that event, He is probably just a mystic, a wise man, maybe a saint, someone to study, but not Who He says He is.

On the other hand, of course, if you take that look at the Bahá'ís and their communities and you see what I have described, then maybe your decision on who Bahá'u'lláh is gets 'heated up' and becomes quite important not only in your life but in the lives of every individual on this planet.

No, it's not just new teachings, though they are powerful and energizing. It is the fact that the Promise of all Ages has showed up, the Return of Christ has occurred and there is a fresh outpouring of Divine guidance in the person of Bahá'u'lláh, the *"Father"* of all mankind. Bahá'u'lláh said that God had given many wonderful *"gifts"* to humankind, but: ***"That which is preeminent above all other gifts, is incorruptible in nature, and pertaineth to God Himself, is the gift of Divine Revelation. Every bounty conferred by the Creator upon man, be it material or spiritual, is subservient unto this.***

" It is, in its essence, and will ever so remain, the Bread which cometh down from Heaven. It is God's supreme testimony, the clearest evidence of His truth, the sign of His consummate bounty, the token of His all-encompassing mercy, the proof of His most loving providence, the symbol of His most perfect grace. He hath, indeed, partaken of this highest gift of God who hath recognized His Manifestation in this Day." (Bahá'u'lláh, *Gleanings*, 1939, 195)

QUESTION: The truth is I'm still uncertain about what you are saying. It all sounds so new, so unlikely, and I've been wondering, how all this could have been happening without my notice. As I said before, why didn't I hear about it until now? Why, if it's so great, hasn't it been in the news, why isn't the world taking notice? Oh, I heard you when you said that the world didn't take notice of the Christian Faith for several hundred years and more, but these are modern times, with instant communication, a thousand newspapers and books and every form of media. I just don't get it!

RESPONSE: To help you to know the actual growth and spread of the Bahá'í Faith, statistics released in the year 2000 (www.bahai.us) showed the following: The Bahá'í Faith was established in 190 countries of the world. It had nearly 6,000,000 adherents. There were 2,112 races, tribes and ethnic groups represented and literature existed in 803 languages. National Spiritual Assemblies existed in 182 countries. Local Spiritual Assemblies were counted at 12,591 and Bahá'ís lived in 129,949 localities around the globe. The Encyclopedia Britannica, in 1996, referred to the Bahá'í Faith as the most widespread religion in the world, save for Christianity.

And maybe this will help. We are probably at the point, here in the twenty-first century of the Common Era, where the world will begin to take proper notice of the Bahá'í Faith and the Bahá'í community, which will soon be too large to ignore and, more importantly, so effective in changing lives and building vibrant, successful communities, that the world will be quite ready to notice and, perhaps, to emulate. That is our hope, that we can provide a guiding light, a successful example of the presence of unity in the world. We believe that this 'presence of unity' will draw the people of earth to the long-promised time of resurrection and reunion that, in some way, all Faiths have predicted and prophesied.

As I've said before, the Christian community was extremely small and little noticed in the great Roman Empire for several hundred years. Witness the fact that (with only one or two minor exceptions) not one well-known person was a Christian for more than three centuries, not one poet or scholar, nor general, governor nor anyone of note. But then, suddenly, Christianity broke out into the world's attention and within a short few decades, everyone seemed to know about it.

I'll bet some people who were around in 100 AD said what you said, that they just couldn't understand, if the Christian Faith was so great, why hadn't they heard about it and why wasn't it being talked about in the Roman Senate? You can test this with your own memory. Can you think of a well-known Roman or Greek person who became Christian in the first three centuries after the beginning of the Christian Faith, other than St. Paul and the Apostles and companions of Christ?

My own answer to this question is this: When you brought this up before, I said that all I can figure out is that this is 'God's way of doing things,' slow and steady, person by person, transformed life by transformed life, toward new spiritually empowered, task-oriented communities and finally, on to a broadly changed, new and better world. Christians, if they understand the history of the early Church, know what I am talking about. The very thing that happened in early Christianity is happening again in the world as we speak, within Bahá'í individuals and Bahá'í communities. Take a look at the Bahá'ís and the Bahá'í Community to see whether or not I am telling a true story. I assure you that I am, but nothing beats finding out for yourself.

It's easy enough to do. Reading this book and entering into this conversation is just a first step. Next, find the Bahá'ís and take a look at them. If you have a computer or access to one, log onto www.bahai.org for complete information. As a last resort, go to the section called 'Connecting with the author,' which appears just before the bibliography near the end of the book.

Finally, as to your expressed confusion, I think it might be helpful to read more about something called 'progressive revelation,' which is a new way of looking at history and trying to understand history in a new and radically different way. When you understand what Bahá'u'lláh means by 'progressive revelation,' you will begin to see why the Bahá'ís are so excited about the prospect of human unity expressed by a Bahá'í phrase - 'one God, one planet, one people'. To find out more about progressive revelation, consult my previous book: *Questions from Christians: About Bahá'u'lláh and the Bahá'í Faith.*

To close this chapter, here are three prayers, one from Bahá'u'lláh, followed by two from 'Abdu'l-Bahá, His Son. I promised you these prayers from 'Abdu'l-Bahá and I think you may enjoy them quite a bit.

First from Bahá'u'lláh:

"O my God! O my God! Unite the hearts of Thy servants, and reveal to them Thy great purpose. May they follow Thy commandments and abide in Thy law. Help them, O God, in their endeavor, and grant them strength to serve Thee. O God! Leave them not to themselves, but guide their steps by the light of Thy knowledge, and cheer their hearts by Thy love. Verily, Thou art their Helper and their Lord." (Bahá'u'lláh: *Bahá'í Prayers*: 2002, 206)

And from 'Abdu'l-Bahá:

"O my God! O my God! Verily, I invoke Thee and supplicate before Thy threshold, asking Thee that all Thy mercies may descend upon these souls. Specialize them for Thy favor and Thy truth.

"O Lord! Unite and bind together the hearts, join in accord all the souls, and exhilarate the spirits through the signs of Thy sanctity and oneness. O Lord! Make these faces radiant through the light of Thy oneness. Strengthen the loins of Thy servants in the service of Thy kingdom.

"O Lord, Thou possessor of infinite mercy! O Lord of forgiveness and pardon! Forgive our sins, pardon our shortcomings, and cause us to turn to the kingdom of Thy clemency, invoking the kingdom of might and power, humble at Thy shrine and submissive before the glory of Thine evidences.

"O Lord God! Make us as waves of the sea, as flowers of the garden, united, agreed through the bounties of Thy love. O Lord! Dilate the breasts through the signs of Thy oneness, and make all mankind as stars shining from the same height of glory, as perfect fruits growing upon Thy tree of life.

"Verily, Thou art the Almighty, the Self-Subsistent, the Giver, the Forgiving, the Pardoner, the Omniscient, the One Creator." ('Abdu'l-Bahá: *Bahá'í Prayers*, 2002, 204-205)

Keeping in mind that so many of the world's peoples are caught up in the destructive passions and false gods of racism, materialism, unbridled nationalism and sexism and are deprived of any idea or any hope of unity with other cultures, religions and races, this following prayer of 'Abdul-Baha seems directly keyed to the needs of the masses of people around the world.

"O Thou, my God, Who guidest the seeker to the pathway that leadeth aright, Who deliverest the lost and blinded soul out of the wastes of perdition, Thou Who bestowest upon the sincere great bounties and favours, Who guardest the frightened within Thine impregnable refuge, Who answerest, from Thine all-highest horizon, the cry of those who cry out unto Thee. Praised be Thou, O my Lord! Thou hast guided the distracted out of the death of unbelief, and hast brought those who draw nigh unto Thee to the journey's goal, and hast rejoiced the assured among Thy servants by granting them their most cherished desires, and hast, from Thy Kingdom of beauty, opened before the faces of those who yearn after Thee the gates of reunion, and hast rescued them from the fires of deprivation and loss - so that they hastened unto Thee and gained Thy presence, and arrived at Thy welcoming door, and received of gifts an abundant share.

"O my Lord, they thirsted, Thou didst lift to their parched lips the waters of reunion. O Tender One, Bestowing One, Thou didst calm their pain with the balm of Thy bounty and grace, and didst heal their ailments with the sovereign medicine of Thy compassion. O Lord, make firm their feet on Thy straight path, make wide for them the needle's eye, and cause them, dressed in royal robes, to walk in glory for ever and ever.

"Verily art Thou the Generous, the Ever-Giving, the Precious, the Most Bountiful. There is none other God but Thee, the Mighty, the Powerful, the Exalted, the Victorious." ('Abdu'l-Bahá, 1978, *Selections from the Writings of 'Abdu'l-Bahá*, 317)

CHAPTER 2

Bahá'u'lláh's Spiritual and Social Teachings; What they could Mean for Christians and the World

QUESTION: My first thought about Bahá'u'lláh's 'teachings' is that Christians don't need any new teachings. If they would only live up to the ones they already have, this world would be a much better place.

RESPONSE: I think you are right, or mostly right. Bahá'u'lláh Himself said many times that if the teachings of any of the world's great religions were actually followed carefully and well, this world would already have become a 'Paradise.'

The reason I said you were 'mostly right' is that I can think of many of Bahá'u'lláh's teachings that are not in the Christian revelation. Of the many, here are two: The abolition of human slavery and the equality of men and women.

QUESTION: Are you trying to minimize or put down the Christian religion!? I thought you said that Bahá'ís would never do such a thing?

RESPONSE: They wouldn't. And I wouldn't. Jesus Himself said: *"I still have many things to say to you, but you cannot bear them now."* (John 16:12-15) You and I know that Jesus Christ would, most certainly, have been against slavery. But the New Testament does not forbid slavery. In fact, St. Paul tells 'bondservants' (read 'slaves'), *"Bondservants, be obedient to those who are your masters"* (Ephesians 6:5)

Should we wonder why Jesus didn't speak on this? We don't know, but it seems obvious to me that His explanation in John 16:12 is sufficient: *"I still have many things to say to you, but you cannot bear them now."*

Human slavery was so widespread that humanity at that time was simply not ready for a teaching that it must be abolished. The people of Jesus' time would not have been able to conceive of a world without slavery. St. Paul, Christ's chief disciple after the original twelve and His major interpreter, sent a Christian, who was a slave - Onesimus - back to his master after he had escaped. While he told the master to receive him as a 'brother,' he pointedly did not ask the master to free him. (Philemon: 8-14) It is one of the most unfortunate moments in Christian history, that slave masters in the American South constantly used this biblical reference to justify human slavery.

QUESTION: But Christians believe that it is the Spirit of Truth that Christ promised to send that *"will guide you into all truth"* that will allow us to discover needed truths, for example, of the horror of slavery. And slavery was abolished, mainly through Christian pressure.

RESPONSE: Well, again, yes and no. It certainly was abolished in Christian nations first (it still goes on in the Sudan, for example) but not without every Christian denomination in the Southern United States breaking away during the Civil War and supporting slavery. They quoted the Bible passages I just mentioned above (twisting their meaning) to support the idea that slavery was, in fact, divinely ordained! Only the Quakers stood firm on this issue.

Early Christians often exerted pressure upon rulers for more humane treatment of slaves, although this was sadly lacking in the pre-civil war American South. Largely from Christian influence, Roman rulers passed a law in 337 AD outlawing the murder of slaves, but even then there was no outcry for the abolishment of slavery, for people could not yet, as Christ said, hear this truth. As late at the 1860's, slavery was still just assumed to be part of the normal landscape and Christian families with any wealth could own slaves, just as they had for 1,500 years.

You mentioned the *"Spirit of Truth"* that Christ promised would appear. It is important for you to know that Bahá'u'lláh said He was that *"Spirit of Truth."* Let's first consult what Christ said, then Bahá'u'lláh. First Christ: *"I still have many things to say to you, but you cannot bear them now. However, when He, the Spirit of truth, has come, He will guide you into all truth; for He will not speak on His own authority, but whatever He hears He will speak; and He will tell you things to come. He will glorify Me, for He will take of what is Mine and declare it to you."* (John 16:12-15)

This is what Bahá'u'lláh said: *"Lo! He Who is the Ruler is come. Step out from behind the veil in the name of thy Lord, He Who layeth low the necks of all men. Proclaim then unto all mankind the glad-tidings of this mighty, this glorious Revelation. Verily, He Who is the Spirit of Truth is come to guide you unto all truth. He speaketh not as prompted by His own self, but as bidden by Him Who is the All-Knowing, the All-Wise.*

"Say, this is the One Who hath glorified the Son [that is, Jesus] **and hath exalted His Cause. Cast away, O peoples of the earth, that which ye have and take fast hold of that which ye are bidden by the All-Powerful, He Who is the Bearer of the Trust of God."** (Bahá'u'lláh: *Tablets of Bahá'u'lláh*, 1978, 12)

The Bahá'í Writings also call unreservedly for recognition of the equality of women and men, and for full 'gender equality' in all areas. Neither Jesus, Muhammad, or Buddha, nor any of the previous Manifestations until Bahá'u'lláh said much if anything about this now all-important social topic. Does this mean that these earlier religions are deficient? It certainly does not! Does it mean that they are somehow less good? Definitely not! What it means is what Jesus said: That a Manifestation teaches as much as men and women are able to hear when He comes. He gives to the world as much as they can 'bear,' but does not try to teach them what they certainly could not hear, understand or accept.

To mention just one more instance of the 'newness' of Bahá'u'lláh's teachings, He forbids consumption of alcohol and drugs (of course, this does not include prescription drugs). Jesus said nothing of this and the only instance of understanding His attitude toward wine is that He turned water into wine at a wedding feast at Cana. It had to have been real wine, because the New Testament records that the guests said something like: "Why did you save the best until last?" Also, St. Paul advises one of his disciples to drink wine for medicinal purposes. But here is the important point: Is one religion better than another because it has a teaching that an earlier one did not have? No, not at all.

That is what Bahá'u'lláh is trying to get us to understand. When a Manifestation comes at any time in human history, His teachings are *exactly* what are needed for that time and those people. Bahá'u'lláh reminds us that there is only one God, not many. One and the same God sent each and every one of the Manifestations.

Therefore, none of what we have been talking about means that the Christian Faith is deficient or that Christ would not have been for equality of men and women and against alcohol consumption and slavery. Rather, it means only what Christ said, in effect, I have additional teachings and lessons that I would like to tell you now, but you wouldn't even be able to understand them. He then said: **"However, when He, the Spirit of truth, has come, He will guide you into all truth"** (John 16:13)

Who is this **"Spirit of Truth"**? Bahá'u'lláh said not just once (as in the quote above) but numerous times that He was that **"Spirit of Truth"** of whom Jesus spoke and promised. Bahá'u'lláh said very directly that He was the return of the Spirit of Christ and told the people of the world that Christ was now to be seen again **"in My person."** Most important, He said that He was the appearance in history of **"the Father"** of all mankind.

Another quote about the ***"Spirit of Truth"*** is taken from a letter Bahá'u'lláh wrote to the Kings of Christian nations: ***"O kings of Christendom! Heard ye not the saying of Jesus, the Spirit of God, 'I go away, and come again unto you'? Wherefore, then, did ye fail, when He did come again unto you in the clouds of heaven, to draw nigh unto Him, that ye might behold His face, and be of them that attained His Presence? In another passage He saith: 'When He, the Spirit of Truth, is come, He will guide you into all truth.' And yet, behold how, when He did bring the truth, ye refused to turn your faces towards Him, and persisted in disporting yourselves with your pastimes and fancies."*** (Bahá'u'lláh, *Gleanings*, 1939, 246)

Bahá'u'lláh said that this ***"Father,"*** this ***"Spirit of Truth"*** would shower upon all the men and women of the entire earth, the knowledge, the teachings and the spiritual power needed to build a free, united, peaceful world that could appropriately be called 'the Kingdom of God on earth.' Jesus prayed for this in the 'Lord's Prayer' and Bahá'ís believe that it is to be realized in the period of history in which we are now living.

QUESTION: I'll grant you that there may be new teachings, but a Christian can come to realization of those same teachings through prayer and careful study of the scriptures, if they will just be true to the Spirit of Jesus.

RESPONSE: That's true. But even today Christians don't agree, for example, on the equality of men and women, do they?

QUESTION: True Christians do, I believe.

RESPONSE: I'd have to agree with that, but let me ask you whether Christians who believe that men and women are *not* equal would agree that they are not true Christians? We know they would disagree with that, to the extreme. And, the fact remains that during the United States Civil War, almost all Christian Churches and Christians in the Southern United States broke away, using sources in the Bible (incorrectly) to support their belief in slavery, even claiming slavery to be 'God's Will.'

Many Christians even today use biblical verses to support paternalism, male superiority and male dominance over women. It might be worth mentioning that many Muslims do the same thing, even today, quoting sacred scriptures from the Qur'án (narrowly and intolerantly) to support the same things.

The point I am making is that Bahá'ís could not experience this confusion or disunity, simply because Bahá'u'lláh and His Son 'Abdu'l-Bahá spoke out so forcefully, clearly and directly on those issues and many others. No Bahá'í group could 'break away,' saying that we don't want to believe in the oneness of humanity, or the need to do away with racial prejudice or gender inequality in our community. I'm not saying that Bahá'ís are perfect. Indeed, individual Bahá'ís and Bahá'í communities always need to 'grow' in their recognition of the full meaning of their teachings. What I *am* saying is that no Bahá'í Community or national Bahá'í group could get away with being 'for' gender inequality or racial prejudice or being against interracial marriage.

QUESTION: Well, I can't help wondering why you didn't just learn these teachings and remain within the Christian Faith, remaining true to Christ?

RESPONSE: Maybe the understanding that we need here should come from Jesus. When He was asked why His teachings couldn't just be added to the wonderful Jewish traditions and religion, do you remember what He said? I know you do. He said: ***"And no one puts new wine into old wineskins..."*** (Luke 5:37) That must have been hard for Jewish ears to hear from Jesus, but it was nevertheless true. The same is true today. This 'new wine' cannot really be contained in the 'old wineskins' or bottles of tradition and old institutions.

No less important, I suspect that Peter, Paul, John and others felt that they remained true to their Jewish Faith, even while following Jesus; in that same way, I feel true and real in my commitment to Jesus Christ today, as much so as when I fell on my knees at fifteen to give my life to Him.

QUESTION: I'm ready to hear what Bahá'u'lláh's other teachings are but you should know that I still believe I have all that I need. But as we said before, it's better to have an open mind and to be willing to investigate. After all, if those around Christ had not had an open mind, they would have missed His Truth and Reality.

RESPONSE: Your statement about an open mind is really important, and I'm glad that you are open to investigation and discussion. Let's actually start with Jesus. As I understand it, His most important teaching was that He had appeared as the Word of God, that He was the one who would be, as He said: ***"Sitting at the right hand of Power*** [that is, God]." When Jesus said this, He was at His trial for blasphemy and the so-called criminal and blasphemous acts with which He had been charged. However, Jesus knew and we now know that He was possessed of the power of God, that He was God's ***"only begotten Son," "the Way, the Truth, and the Life,"*** and that ***"no man cometh unto the Father but by Me."*** Finally, most importantly, Jesus taught that the sacrifice of His life brought salvation to humanity.

Now, and it's not a contrast at all, let's look at Bahá'u'lláh's most important teaching: It was that He, ***"the Father"*** had come, that He was the Return of the Spirit of Christ - the actual reappearance of Christ ***"in my person"*** - that He was the ***"Spirit of Truth"*** that Christ had said would ***"guide you into all truth."***

Bahá'u'lláh said: ***"Thou art He, O my God, Who hath raised me up at Thy behest, and bidden me to occupy Thy seat, and to summon all men to the court of Thy mercy. It is Thou Who hast commanded me to tell out the things Thou didst destine for them in the Tablet of Thy decree and didst inscribe with the pen of Thy Revelation, and Who hast enjoined on me the duty of kindling the fire of Thy love in the hearts of Thy servants, and of drawing all the peoples of the earth nearer to the habitation of Thy throne."*** (Bahá'u'lláh, *Prayers and Meditations*, 1938, 107)

Also, ***"Call out to Zion, O Carmel, and announce the joyful tidings: He that was hidden from mortal eyes is come!"*** (Bahá'u'lláh, *Gleanings*, 1939, 16) and ***"Speed out of your sepulchers. How long will ye sleep? The second blast hath been blown on the trumpet.***

On whom are ye gazing? This is your Lord, the God of Mercy." (Bahá'u'lláh, *Gleanings*, 1939, 44)

He told the people of the world, *"Fix your gaze upon Him Who is the Temple of God amongst men. He, in truth, hath offered up His life as a ransom for the redemption of the world."* (Bahá'u'lláh, *Gleanings*, 1939, 315)

QUESTION: Really, I have to stop you there. Christ died for our sins and provided, once and for all time, the 'ransom' for the redemption of the world. Christians cannot accept that anything further is needed in terms of redemption.

RESPONSE: I realize that this is the Christian position. What Bahá'u'lláh asks of us is to continue our 'core belief,' but to widen it, expand it, to see that there is a work of a 'Greater God' in history. He asks us to realize that what Christians believe about Christ's redemptive power is true not only for Christ but that all the other Manifestations have also provided redemption through their sufferings and, in some cases, their sacrificial deaths.

Whenever God's full Presence, His 'Word' appears in human history, God is acting to 'redeem' us from our worst mistakes and to 'save' us from our folly and our unwillingness to see the truth. Each and every Manifestation, says Bahá'u'lláh, provides this ransom and redemption and, as well, personal salvation. By the way, Bahá'u'lláh teaches that God will continue to send Manifestations of his Presence into the world and indicated that this would happen about every thousand years. He also said very clearly that there would not be another Manifestation for a full period of one-thousand years from the date of His declaration (1853), which would be some time later than 2853 of the CE.

Bahá'u'lláh referred to Himself as: *"Him Who is the Word of Truth amidst you."* (Bahá'u'lláh, *Gleanings*, 1939, 316) and advised His followers to *"Keep your gaze centered on Him Who is the Sovereign Word of Truth: place your whole reliance upon Him, and beg of Him to destine for you what is meet and fitting."* (Bahá'u'lláh: *Compilations: Vol. II, Trustworthiness*, 332)

Finally, echoing Jesus' statement about being seated at *"the right hand of Power* [that is, God]," Bahá'u'lláh said He came *"from the invisible heaven, bearing the banner 'He doeth whatsoever He willeth' and is accompanied by hosts of power and authority..."* (Bahá'u'lláh: *Tablets of Bahá'u'lláh*, 1978, 108)

And, just as Christ said: *"No man cometh unto the Father but by me"* Bahá'u'lláh said: *"No man can obtain everlasting life, unless he embraceth the truth of this inestimable, this wondrous, and sublime Revelation."* Bahá'u'lláh, *Gleanings*, 1939, 183) and while Christ said: *"If you have seen me you have seen the Father,"* Bahá'u'lláh said: *"If it be your wish, O people, to know God and to discover the greatness of His might, look, then, upon Me..."* (Bahá'u'lláh, *Gleanings*, 1939, 272)

As to salvation and the sacrifice made by all the Manifestations and in this day by Bahá'u'lláh, He said: *"We, verily, have come for your sakes, and have borne the misfortunes of the world for your salvation. Flee ye the One Who hath sacrificed His life that ye may be quickened? Fear God, O followers of the Spirit (Jesus), and walk not in the footsteps of every divine* [the clergy] *that hath gone far astray... Open the doors of your hearts. He Who is the Spirit (Jesus) verily, standeth before them."* (Bahá'u'lláh: *Proclamation of Bahá'u'lláh*, 1978, 91-92)

He also said: **"Blessed the soul that hath been raised to life through My quickening breath and hath gained admittance into My heavenly Kingdom."** (Bahá'u'lláh: *Tablets of Bahá'u'lláh*, 1978, 16) and in a prayer to God, Bahá'u'lláh speaks of Himself as **"Him Whom Thou hast sacrificed that all the dwellers of Thine earth and heaven may be born anew, and Whom Thou hast cast into prison that mankind may, as a token of Thy bounty and of Thy sovereign might, be released from the bondage of evil passions and corrupt desires."** (Bahá'u'lláh, *Prayers and Meditations*, 1938, 44)

QUESTION: I can agree that the most important teaching of the Christian Faith is that God revealed Himself and His Will in Jesus Christ and manifested salvation to the world through Jesus' sacrifice on the cross, so I guess I can understand why Bahá'ís might see Bahá'u'lláh's coming as the main teaching of their Faith and even why His suffering and imprisonment are important.

But, exactly what are the specific and main teachings of Bahá'u'lláh? Can you spell them out to me in some detail?

RESPONSE: The teachings of Bahá'u'lláh fall into four categories, as I understand them. First, some ideas about God and humanity and the way God reveals His will to humankind and the way He manifests Himself in history. Second, social teachings designed to hasten the building of a new social order that can fittingly be named 'the Kingdom of God on earth' (as envisioned and prayed for by Jesus). Third, laws given by Bahá'u'lláh, such as those governing marriage, the family, burial, abstinence from alcohol and drugs, and other laws. Fourth, teachings and writings about prayer, meditation, fasting and spiritual growth.

QUESTION: Tell me first, if you will, of the Bahá'í teachings about God and man and the way God reveals His will to mankind, although it seems we have just been talking a lot about this subject in the last two chapters, haven't we?

RESPONSE: You are right, so just let me summarize those teachings:

1. **There is only one God**. Several generations ago, we spoke of 'false gods' when we referred to the religions of other peoples and cultures. We tended to think of the God of our religion as 'the True God' and the God of, say, the Muslims or Buddhists as a 'false god.' Some people still think this way but many Christians and others realize the truth of Bahá'u'lláh's teaching that there is and has always been only one God, the Father of us all.

2. **There is only one humankind**. Beneath all the cultures, religions, 'races', ethnic groups, languages, customs, beneath it all, we are one, Bahá'u'lláh tells us. He says it is God's Will that we recognize and enact this oneness. Here is perhaps His most famous quote: ***"The earth is but one country, and mankind its citizens."*** (Bahá'u'lláh, *Gleanings*, 1939, 250) He also said that God's wish, expressed through Him, was to behold ***"the entire human race as one soul and one body."*** (*ibid.*, 214)

3. **This one God has always been lovingly guiding this one humanity in this one place, earth, toward an eventual time in**

history when prophecies of peace and unity would be fulfilled in a 'golden age' or a 'Kingdom of God' on earth.

4. **The way God provides this guidance is first and foremost through sending progressive and successive Manifestations of Himself to earth and its people.**

Bahá'u'lláh said that God *"hath in every age and cycle, in conformity with His transcendent wisdom, sent forth a divine Messenger to revive the dispirited and despondent souls with the living waters of His utterance."* (Bahá'u'lláh: *Tablets of Bahá'u'lláh*, 1978, 161)

He tells us that God *"hath ordained the knowledge of these sanctified Beings to be identical with the knowledge of His own Self. Whoso recognizeth them hath recognized God. Whoso hearkeneth to their call, hath hearkened to the Voice of God, and whoso testifieth to the truth of their Revelation, hath testified to the truth of God Himself.*

"Whoso turneth away from them, hath turned away from God, and whoso disbelieveth in them, hath disbelieved in God. Every one of them is the Way of God that connecteth this world with the realms above, and the Standard of His Truth unto every one in the kingdoms of earth and heaven. They are the Manifestations of God amidst men, the evidences of His Truth, and the signs of His glory." (Bahá'u'lláh, *Gleanings*, 1939, 50)

After ages of promise and prophecy, Bahá'u'lláh reveals that God Himself stepped forth into history: *"He that was hidden from mortal eyes is come! His all-conquering sovereignty is manifest; His all-encompassing splendor is revealed."* (ibid. 16) and *"He Who, from everlasting, had concealed His Face from the sight of creation is now come."* (ibid. 31)

QUESTION: I'm still frankly confused. You told me earlier that Bahá'u'lláh did not claim to be God, but here it seems pretty clear that He did make that claim. It seems contradictory!

RESPONSE: Well, I don't want to repeat everything we discussed in chapters four through seven [these chapters are in the book *Questions from Christians*], so you may want to review them, but both Jesus and Bahá'u'lláh made what seem to be, *at first*, contradictory statements. They both spoke of being 'one' with God, but both also vehemently denied being God. We know now that these statements aren't contradictory at all, but simply are statements that speak of the full Presence of the 'Word of God' that is within them, as well as the fact that they appear in a human form, as Bahá'u'lláh says, **"the human temple."**

The Manifestations are human beings, 'fully man,' as Christian doctrine says, but they also represent God to man in such a full way that to look at them is to see God, to hear them is to hearken to God, to obey them is to obey God. There is a passage just a page or two above that you may want to reread, that speaks to this, which brings us to the fifth, all important aspect of Bahá'u'lláh's teachings.

5. **Bahá'u'lláh represented the fulfillment of mankind's age-long hopes, dreams and prophecies.**

Bahá'u'lláh announced that He was:

First: The Return of Christ and the One Whom Christ called the *"Spirit of Truth."*

Second: The spiritual 'Return' of all of the figures awaited by all the world's religions and cultures. Thus, He is the 'Promise of all Ages.'[5]

Third: The appearance of *"The Father"* of all mankind, come at long last after centuries of hope and expectation. He was, He said, the One Who would empower individual men and women and youth of all humanity to begin to build, finally, a united, peaceful world in which the long-awaited 'Kingdom of God' would be increasingly recognized.

Thus, to summarize: One world, one humanity, and one God, guiding humanity toward an era of fulfillment, by Manifesting Himself to different peoples, in different times and places, then finally stepping forth Himself from behind *"veils"* that had hidden Him. Now, He appears in such a way, as Bahá'u'lláh put it, that mankind cannot mistake His coming.

"Verily I say, this is the Day in which mankind can behold the Face, and hear the Voice, of the Promised One. The Call of God hath been raised, and the light of His countenance hath been lifted up upon men. It behoveth every man to blot out the trace of every idle word from the tablet of his heart, and to gaze, with an open and unbiased mind, on the signs of His Revelation, the proofs of His Mission, and the tokens of His glory. (Bahá'u'lláh, *Gleanings*, 10-11)

---

5 Shoghi Effendi, *God Passes By*. 1944, 58.

And one more important point, especially important to me and to other Bahá'ís from a Christian background, we have found and experienced that if one becomes a Bahá'í, that is, a follower of Bahá'u'lláh, one renews and deepens faith in Christ.

This renewal and 'deepening' occurs when the new believer in Bahá'u'lláh acknowledges not only Faith in Bahá'u'lláh, but also faith in God's other Manifestations of Himself, namely, Moses, Buddha, Zoroaster, Krishna, Christ, Muhammad, Bahá'u'lláh and others. He now sees what he understands as the Spirit of Christ, the pre-existent Word of God at work in all the Manifestations. By this acknowledgment and declaration of faith, the new Bahá'í becomes a 'citizen of the world' and all of human history now belongs to him. All people are 'His people.' The word 'foreign' can no longer be used by him in a spiritual way. He now fully understands the truth of Bahá'u'lláh's words: ***"It is not for him to pride himself who loveth his own country, but rather for him who loveth the whole world. The earth is but one country, and mankind its citizens."*** (ibid. 250)

QUESTION: I'm not sure I understand when you are talking about a new believer in the Bahá'í Faith, by saying: 'all history now belongs to him'. Doesn't history belong to everyone anyway? What do you mean?

RESPONSE: Well, I may be guilty of some exuberance, but a person who becomes a Bahá'í has a 'rush' of realization that all of the religions, the cultures, the ethnic groups of all history are now seen to be a parts of a larger pattern, formed and fashioned by God, with the pattern finally 'making sense' in the coming of Bahá'u'lláh and in His teachings. In this way, all of history *does* belong to this new

Bahá'í. If you would ask any Bahá'í in the world (no matter what background they come from, Hindu, Jewish or Buddhist, for example), they would say that Christ is central to their Bahá'í belief in a way that any Christian would respect and admire.

He sees that all people are his people, that the religions are, in their essence, one. God's purpose is seen in that He has 'progressively' revealed His Will in many places, many times, laying down many prophetic hopes and dreams. Now this Bahá'í feels that he is a 'witness' to a new day in which God has ***"stepped forth"*** into the world with a fresh revelation designed to gather all humankind into the fulfillment of those dreams and the realization of the many prophecies of peace, oneness and unity.

QUESTION: You sound as if you are saying that all people are alike and that all the religions are the same?

RESPONSE: No, not at all, although when people hear the Bahá'í message for the first time, that often seems to be what they hear. However, it is subtle and more meaningful than that. The religions are different, in some ways very different, on the surface and especially in terms of social teachings, given by God for the day in which that Manifestation of God appeared.

When God appeared in the persons of Jesus or Muhammad or Buddha, the needs of the people were different and the social teachings were therefore special and distinct, targeted to the needs of that day. A famous example would be Moses telling the Israelites not to eat pork, which would be dangerous for a desert-living, nomadic people, but not problematic at all in an age of refrigeration.

But, as we have discussed before, if you go below the surface, to the deeper 'core' of any religion, you find great similarity and a zone of true 'oneness.' Not 'sameness' but 'oneness.' The reason you find this oneness is that the next finding you make, at the deepest level of all religions is, not surprisingly, God Himself, Who has been the mover and initiator of all the religions, as Bahá'u'lláh taught.

The religions are different, very different on the surface. Deeper down, similar. At the deepest level, they are 'one.'

Bahá'ís believe God was the motive force and initiator of all the religions by sending into history many Manifestations of His *"own Being."* Bahá'u'lláh spoke of Himself as *"Him Whom Thou hast appointed as the Manifestation of Thine own Being and Thy discriminating Word unto all that are in heaven and on earth, to gather together Thy servants beneath the shade of the Tree of Thy gracious providence."* (Bahá'u'lláh, *Prayers and Meditations*, 1938, 26)

We can realize, first, that the Manifestations, all of them, are not only 'fully man' in the sense of appearing in *"the human Temple"*, but also are God in the sense of the *"Presence"* of God that is within them. Then it becomes easier to understand the following statement of Bahá'u'lláh about the Manifestations (such as Muhammad, Buddha, Jesus, and others):

"It is clear and evident to thee that all the Prophets are the Temples of the Cause of God, Who have appeared clothed in divers attire. If thou wilt observe with discriminating eyes, thou wilt behold Them all abiding in the same tabernacle, soaring in the same heaven, seated upon the same throne, uttering the same speech,

and proclaiming the same Faith." (Bahá'u'lláh, *Gleanings*, 1939, 52) and *"they are all but one person, one soul, one spirit, one being, one revelation."* (Bahá'u'lláh, *Gleanings*, 1939, 54)

QUESTION: What about the 'social teachings' you said each Manifestation gives? What social teachings did Bahá'u'lláh give?

RESPONSE: We always have to remember that Bahá'u'lláh, like Christ, said that He said nothing and did nothing but that which God asked Him to convey to humankind. *"I can utter no word, O my God, unless I be permitted by Thee, and can move in no direction until I obtain Thy sanction. It is Thou, O my God, Who hast called me into being through the power of Thy might, and hast endued me with Thy grace to manifest Thy Cause."* (Bahá'u'lláh, *Prayers and Meditations*, 1938, 208)

With the spiritual confidence that could only come from the realization that God was speaking through Him, He said: *"Neither the hosts of the earth nor those of heaven can keep me back from revealing the things I am commanded to manifest. I have no will before Thy will, and can cherish no desire in the face of Thy desire."* (ibid. 184)

We have already mentioned several of those social teachings, but before we list the others, let us realize that the social teachings of Bahá'u'lláh flow out of the spiritual teachings listed just above, which focus on God's work in history, so let us review:

Bahá'u'lláh teaches that there is only one God, not many Gods, and that all the religions were initiated by this one God, who 'sent' a Messenger or Manifestation of Himself (in the case of the Christian

Faith, that Manifestation was His own *'Son'*). Each of these Manifestations gave teachings, started a religion and empowered individuals and communities to live salvation-changed, renewed lives, thus transforming the earth.

That God has been progressively revealing Himself to man, preparing man for 'the Promised Day' of 'Resurrection' when all humanity would be brought into peace and unity; that Bahá'u'lláh finally appeared on earth, as a Manifestation of God's ***"own Self"*** (Bahá'u'lláh, *Gleanings*, 1939 102), as ***"the Father"*** of all mankind to fulfill past prophecies of all religions and to establish and build the 'Kingdom of God' that would express His Will ***"on earth as it is in heaven."*** (Mt: 6-10)

Based upon these spiritual concepts, the following social teachings are those revealed by Bahá'u'lláh:

1. **Mankind is one.**
Properly speaking, there is only one race, the human race. Science agrees with Bahá'u'lláh's teaching that although there certainly are different ethnic groups, cultures, religions, customs, nevertheless, there is only one race on this earth. Speaking of all humanity, Bahá'u'lláh says: ***"Ye are all the leaves of one tree and the drops of one ocean."*** (Bahá'u'lláh, Tablets *of Bahá'u'lláh*, 1978, 129)

Also: ***"Ye are the fruits of one tree, and the leaves of one branch. Deal ye one with another with the utmost love and harmony, with friendliness and fellowship. He Who is the Day-Star of Truth beareth Me witness! So powerful is the light of unity that it can illuminate the whole earth."*** (Bahá'u'lláh, *Epistle to the Son of the Wolf*, 1979, 14)

2. **All prejudice toward people of other 'races', ethnic groups or cultures must cease.**
The virus of prejudice is beginning to cease within Bahá'í communities across the planet, as Bahá'ís are striving in many practical ways to raise 'prejudice-free children.' We realize and welcome the efforts of Christians, Muslims, Jews and others who are working toward the same goal. Bahá'u'lláh said He gave God's Will for today to mankind and stated God's major wish: ***"He Who is your Lord, the All-Merciful, cherisheth in His heart the desire of beholding the entire human race as one soul and one body."*** Bahá'u'lláh, *Gleanings*, 1939, 214)

However (and this is important) diversity of cultures and customs is appreciated. An interesting footnote to this worldwide plan to wipe out prejudice in Bahá'í communities is that, in elections, if there is a tie between two individuals and one is of a minority, the elected post is automatically awarded to the minority person.

Bahá'ís are seeing success within their communities in this campaign to carry out God's Will for today and they are doing it in such a way as to preserve diversity. Bahá'ís often say: Unity, but with diversity. No one wants enforced, false unity that covers up the beautiful shades of color and the different customs and ways of the many people of earth.

3. **There must be equality between men and women.**
This must happen in our thinking and in our practice. It must be in our methods of childrearing and in our schools, in business and government. It must begin to permeate all that we do. Bahá'u'lláh revealed: ***"Women and men have been and will always be equal in***

the sight of God. The Dawning-Place of the Light of God sheddeth its radiance upon all with the same effulgence. Verily God created women for men, and men for women." (Bahá'u'lláh, Compilations of Compilations, (Women), 2000, 379) It is fascinating to see in the words of Bahá'u'lláh that God did not create one gender for the benefit of the other; rather, both man and woman were created for each other.

Bahá'u'lláh's Son, 'Abdu'l-Bahá said: *"For the world of humanity possesses two wings: man and woman. If one wing remains incapable and defective, it will restrict the power of the other, and full flight will be impossible. Therefore, the completeness and perfection of the human world are dependent upon the equal development of these two wings."* ('Abdu'l-Bahá, The Promulgation of Universal Peace, 1982, 318)

A fascinating exception to this is stated explicitly: Bahá'u'lláh said that if a family has limited income and only one child at a time can be funded for education, the preference must go to the female child to be educated first. He explained that this is because of the woman's all-important role as the first educator of children. But aside from this exception, Bahá'ís are again seeing success worldwide in making discoveries about what the equality of women and men can and should mean. They are acting this out in a 'practical' way in their communities.

4. Extremes of poverty and riches should end.
Toward that goal, the teachings of Bahá'u'lláh foreshadowed by a century the concepts of Social Security, progressive taxation, and profit sharing, among others. The saying of Christ that **"the poor**

you have with you always" (John 12:8) must not be misused to justify 'extreme' poverty nor to permit unlimited acquisition of wealth, Bahá'u'lláh tells us.

He explains that there will always be those who have less and those who have more, but that extremes on both ends must be eliminated. Many of His teachings work in the direction of blunting both extremes of the very poor and the very rich. This would be accomplished, Baha'u'llah explained, by voluntary sharing, rather than by some bureaucratic law. The **"Houses of Justice"** to be elected in every country by Bahá'ís have been given the task, among many others, of insuring the well-being of those less fortunate. However, Bahá'u'lláh teaches that every person should engage in some form of work or trade and that begging or idleness are not to be allowed.

Bahá'u'lláh often encourages His followers to put forth the greatest effort and although Christians, like Jews and Muslims, have been in the forefront of furthering charity and building charitable institutions, some Christians still misuse Christ's statement "The poor you have always with you" (Mt 26:11) to argue against help to the poor. True Christians, Muslims and, of course, the Bahá'ís, all have scripture that admonishes them to render assistance to the poor and dispossessed. This is a particularly strong emphasis in Bahá'í scripture.

Bahá'u'lláh was personally renowned for His extensive works of charity and was known in His early years as 'Father of the Poor.' Nevertheless, He extolled effort, forbade begging and strongly encouraged engaging in work or a profession.

5. Recognizing our oneness and achieving the unity of mankind is the highest, brightest goal for the peoples of the world
Bahá'u'lláh taught that this unification of the human race is the Will of God for today and that it will definitely come to pass in this new era.

6. Unity or oneness must be established in such a way as to respect differences and diversity.
In fact, the unity we seek must even 'celebrate' this diversity and the 'specialness' of various peoples and cultures. Dr. Carl Lee, a Bahá'í friend, feels that we must, in fact, go beyond 'celebration' of diversity. He points out that the International Bahá'í Community, in its statement on 'The Prosperity of Humankind' enjoins us to recognize that diversity has an absolutely critical role in providing the 'social genetic diversity' that is needed for the survival and flourishing of mankind.

Bahá'ís speak of 'unity with diversity' to remind ourselves that no one would want to have or to accept a sterile 'unity' in which our wonderful differences, our beautiful and stunning diversity would be lost or swallowed up in some shallow, half-baked concept of 'oneness.'

'Abdu'l-Bahá said: *"Let us look rather at the beauty in diversity, the beauty of harmony, and learn a lesson from the vegetable creation. If you beheld a garden in which all the plants were the same as to form, colour and perfume, it would not seem beautiful to you at all, but, rather, monotonous and dull. The garden which is pleasing to the eye and which makes the heart glad, is the garden in which are growing side by side flowers of every hue, form and perfume, and the joyous contrast of colour is what makes for charm and beauty."* ('Abdu'l-Bahá, *Paris Talks*, 1995, [1912], 52-53)

7. **The people of the world should adopt a universal language.**
To insure our diversity, every child on the planet should learn two languages, the language of her or his own culture and people and the universal language. This universal language would be chosen by the people of the world, meeting in a gathering, perhaps at the United Nations, or some other future world forum. Bahá'u'lláh advised the Kings and rulers of the world, as well as the people of the world, ***"to adopt one of the existing languages or a new one to be taught to children in schools throughout the world, and likewise one script. Thus the whole earth will come to be regarded as one country."*** (Bahá'u'lláh, *Tablets of Bahá'u'lláh*, 1978, 22)

In another place, Bahá'u'lláh said: ***"The day is approaching when all the peoples of the world will have adopted one universal language and one common script. When this is achieved, to whatsoever city a man may journey, it shall be as if he were entering his own home."*** Bahá'u'lláh, *Gleanings*, 1939, 249-250)

8. **The peoples of the world and their governments should meet together to vote upon and freely choose a united form of planetary government.**
This should not be something forced upon them, or foisted upon them, but something they would freely choose. Bahá'ís around the world are themselves ready for this, to a person, and are spreading the idea of world unity.

From the Revelation of Bahá'u'lláh: ***"The Great Being,*** [that is, God] *wishing to reveal the prerequisites of the peace and tranquillity of the world and the advancement of its peoples, hath written: The time must come when the imperative necessity for the holding of a vast, an all-embracing assemblage of men will be universally realized. The rulers and kings of the earth must needs attend it, and, participating in its deliberations, must consider such ways and means as will lay the foundations of the world's Great Peace amongst men. Such a peace demandeth that the Great Powers should resolve, for the sake of the tranquillity of the peoples of the earth, to be fully reconciled among themselves.*

"Should any king take up arms against another, all should unitedly arise and prevent him. If this be done, the nations of the world will no longer require any armaments, except for the purpose of preserving the security of their realms and of maintaining internal order within their territories. This will ensure the peace and composure of every people, government and nation." (Bahá'u'lláh, *Gleanings*, 1939, 249) Note: This teaching about unity and no longer needing armaments is paramount in importance. Why? Because the trillions of dollars that are poured into armaments each decade are more than enough to materially transform the planet, bringing greater access to food, shelter, health and education to every man, woman and child on earth. A world without these armaments expenditures would be a world greatly changed in two to three generations.

9. **Science and religion must agree.**
In much of the Nineteenth century and nearly all of the Twentieth, religion and science have tended to disagree or even be enemies. A

well-known book was written in the early years of the Twentieth Century speaking of the 'warfare' between science and religion. Bahá'u'lláh said we must strive to realize that faith and reason can, should and must live together in our minds. Faith is not the turning off of reason, and reason is not the shunning of Faith. Our minds are such that we can accommodate and integrate both of these great human faculties. Doing so will lead to great progress as we negotiate the Twenty-First century.

This is what Bahá'u'lláh's Son, 'Abdu'l-Bahá said: *"Religion and science are the two wings upon which man's intelligence can soar into the heights, with which the human soul can progress. It is not possible to fly with one wing alone! Should a man try to fly with the wing of religion alone, he would quickly fall into the quagmire of superstition, whilst on the other hand, with the wing of science alone, he would also make no progress, but fall into the despairing slough of materialism."*

'Abdu'l-Bahá also says in that same passage that in many ways the teachings of the world's religions *"have fallen...out of harmony with the true principles of the teaching they represent and with the scientific discoveries of the time."* ('Abdu'l-Bahá, *Paris Talks*, 1995, 43)

10. **Universal education for every child on the planet.**
Today, in lesser-developed countries, only about one third of the children receive anything approaching basic education. When you consider female children in the poorest of the developing countries, nearly sixty per-cent have inadequate or no education. Bahá'u'lláh says that unity and peace cannot possibly occur until and unless we change the education level of females and also guarantee a basic education to every child on the planet. Bahá'í communities, wherever

they are, are moving in this direction, teaching that all children must be educated and emphasizing the education of female children, which is often not carried out adequately in many developing countries. Indeed, it was not done to an appropriate extent in the culture of the United States just two or three generations ago!

11. Every man, woman and child on this planet must utilize their minds in what Bahá'u'lláh called 'Independent Investigation' to seek out the truth for their lives.
This is last in the list, but certainly not least, and it should be first in one sense, as Bahá'u'lláh talked of it so often and also because it is so crucial to the way in which we collect, receive, and use information. It is Bahá'u'lláh's teaching, His injunction, that we must honor teachers, priests, ministers, parents, but not let them or anyone in authority interfere with our right and obligation to find out for ourselves the truth of any matter.

We can and should get advice, opinion, guidance, especially from parents and teachers, but in the end, Bahá'u'lláh says, it is up to us to decide the truth for ourselves and to make decisions from within, rather than on the basis of some form of external coercion. This is a quote from Bahá'u'lláh's son, 'Abdu'l-Bahá, on this subject:

"Furthermore, know ye that God has created in man the power of reason, whereby man is enabled to investigate reality. God has not intended man to imitate blindly his fathers and ancestors. He has endowed him with mind, or the faculty of reasoning, by the exercise of which he is to investigate and discover the truth, and that which he finds real and true he must accept. He must not be an imitator or blind follower of any soul. He must not rely

implicitly upon the opinion of any man without investigation; nay, each soul must seek intelligently and independently, arriving at a real conclusion and bound only by that reality." ('Abdu'l-Bahá, *The Promulgation of Universal Peace*, 1982, 291)

There are other social teachings, but this is a good sampling and, as you can see, all of Bahá'u'lláh's teachings - Bahá'ís believe them to be the Will of God - center around the idea of the oneness of mankind and flow out of the idea that God has again Manifested Himself in the Person of Bahá'u'lláh, appearing in our current time as **"The Father"** of all mankind, to draw us together into a unity and oneness that has been the dream of prophet and poet alike.

QUESTION: You said there were also 'laws' that Bahá'u'lláh gave? I guess you realize that we talked once before about the fact that Christianity is not a religion of laws. I do remember that you pointed out that Jesus did give several laws, including one regarding divorce and, of course, He gave the Great Commandment and a commandment is a law. And, now that we have had that discussion, I do remember that Jesus said: **"If you love Me, keep My commandments."** (John 14:15) But for the most part, the Christian Faith does not have many laws.[6] What are the laws of Bahá'u'lláh?

RESPONSE: Yes, Bahá'u'lláh actually gave a complete code of laws, but said this about these laws: **"Think not that We have revealed unto you a mere code of laws. Nay, rather, We have unsealed the**

---

6 One reader of this book, Rev. Barbara Berry-Bailey, points out that the Christian Faith fully subscribes to the Jewish Ten Commandments, which are clearly 'Laws' that Christians must obey.

choice Wine with the fingers of might and power." (Bahá'u'lláh, *Gleanings*, 1939, 332) He also said: **"O ye peoples of the world! Know assuredly that My commandments are the lamps of My loving providence among My servants, and the keys of My mercy for My creatures."** (ibid. 331)

Among these laws are laws governing marriage, inheritance, abstinence from alcohol and drugs, means of burial and numerous others that you can learn about as you begin to study the Bahá'í Faith and the Revelation that is seen and witnessed in the life and writings of Bahá'u'lláh. Just as Christians do not see the Great Commandment of Jesus as coming from a human person, but from God, likewise, Bahá'ís see these laws as coming from God and constituting God's plan not only for individuals but for newly transformed human communities as well as the regeneration and revitalization of the entire planet.

QUESTION: That's just my problem! You speak of 'the writings' of Bahá'u'lláh as if they were God speaking. I don't understand that and I certainly find it hard to accept.

RESPONSE: We've spoken about this before, but in the time of Jesus, it must have been difficult, even for the disciples, to realize that when Jesus spoke, they were, in effect, listening to God. Later, after one them made the discovery that all but Judas would acknowledge, that Jesus was the 'Son of God', all of them realized that they were hearing the Will of God spoken to them through Jesus.

Likewise, there will be an evolution here for the people of the world, person by person, to realize first that the ideas being set forth by Bahá'u'lláh are, in fact, the very concepts needed to bring the world into unity. Then, as they - and you - begin the task to decide Who Bahá'u'lláh is, they will slowly, I believe surely, begin to realize that when Bahá'u'lláh speaks, one is hearing, as He said: ***"The Voice of God."*** It still comes back to that question, doesn't it? Who is Bahá'u'lláh? Madman, charlatan? Or, just perhaps, He is Who He said He is, the Return of Christ and the **'*Father*'** of all mankind.

In this regard, remember that earlier quote from Jesus where He says that He only taught what the Father had given to Him. He had innate divine knowledge. It is the same with Bahá'u'lláh, Who often spoke of Himself as a **'*Pen*'** in the Hand of God, so as to say that it was God Who was doing the writing while He was no more than the **'*Pen*'** of God. ***"Thus biddeth you the Lord of creation, the movement of Whose Pen hath revolutionized the soul of mankind. Know ye from what heights your Lord, the All-Glorious is calling?"*** Bahá'u'lláh, *Gleanings*, 1939, 139) We have no knowledge of Jesus having ever attended school. In the case of Bahá'u'lláh, we know most certainly that He did not attend any formal school, at any age, as a child or as an adult.

QUESTION: Let me think about that one. I need to understand what Bahá'u'lláh is saying on several levels. It will take me some time. Meanwhile, what about the final category of teachings you spoke of? Teachings about prayer and meditation and fasting? I guess you know that not all Christians fast?

RESPONSE: Many Protestant Churches do not emphasize fasting, but some do. Most Catholics and Eastern Orthodox Christians fast, as you know. Some Protestants, Evangelicals and others also fast.

As far as I can figure it out, the only reason many Protestants don't fast is that early Protestants were simply trying to distinguish themselves from Catholics in their de-emphasis of fasting.

In my Methodist upbringing, fasting was almost never mentioned. I learned later that many other denominations and branches of Christianity *do* fast. In the case of the Bahá'í Faith, fasting is practiced and required by Bahá'u'lláh as part of the code of laws He gave to the world.

All Bahá'ís who are not too young, too old or too ill or who must work in extremely demanding physical occupations, fast every year just prior to the Bahá'í New Year, which falls on the first day of Spring (the Vernal Equinox, usually March 21.) During the period of fasting, which lasts 19 days, Bahá'ís fast between sunrise and sunset each day. This means, of course, that they can take food and water before sunrise and after sunset. This fasting period serves the same purpose that it serves in Christianity, Islam, or Judaism, namely, for spiritual deepening and renewal. It may also have a beneficial physical effect as well, but is mainly for growth of the spirit.

Finally, this is how Jesus instructed His disciples to fast: ***"But you, when you fast, anoint your head and wash your face, so that you do not appear to men to be fasting, but to your Father who is in the secret place; and your Father who sees in secret will reward you openly."*** (Matt 6:17-19)

Bahá'u'lláh also spoke many times about prayer, the need to pray, and the rewards of prayer and how necessary prayer is to our spiritual growth. I hope you have been enjoying the prayers of Bahá'u'lláh and His son, 'Abdu'l-Bahá, that I have placed at the end of each chapter. The ones at the end of this chapter will be two prayers about the nature of prayer.

Bahá'u'lláh did give a commandment to His followers that they pray at least once each day and revealed special prayers for this purpose. All Bahá'ís are obliged to pray one of these few prayers each day and are strongly encouraged to develop a life of devotion, meditation and prayer as part of their spiritual discipline and life plan.

QUESTION: Any other teachings of Bahá'u'lláh?

RESPONSE: Do you remember me telling you that there are many thousands of documents, notes, letters, epistles, and books from the ***'Pen'*** of Bahá'u'lláh? I could not begin to give you the wealth of what Bahá'u'lláh called ***"the ocean of my words.***" I believe I have hit only the 'high spots' of Bahá'u'lláh's teachings. For the rest, you have a glorious opportunity to investigate and to discover for yourself.

I remember how beautiful the moment was in my life when I first found Christ for myself and accepted Him into my life. And I can remember very well, too, when I realized that, for me, Bahá'u'lláh was the Return of my Jesus. To quote a hymn of my youth: 'How precious did that Grace appear, when first I did believe.'

Several new books or Tablets from Bahá'u'lláh have been translated and published in the Twenty-First Century and more will be seen over the decades ahead. Bahá'ís believers and scholars will be eagerly anticipating these developments.

I believe there are very many other teachings, mostly of a spiritual nature, **"*pearls*"** as Bahá'u'lláh called them, from that **"*ocean.*"** You can discover these 'pearls' for yourself and if it happens as it happened with me, it will be the discovery of your lifetime and a surprise beyond description.

Here is a summary of the teachings of Bahá'u'lláh, which I have offered to you for your thought, reflection, prayer and study:

1. The teachings about His own coming as the Return of the Spirit of Jesus Christ and also as **"The Father"** of all mankind and the 'Promise of All Ages.'
2. Teachings about the Oneness of God and the Oneness of the Manifestations of God.
3. Teachings about 'progressive revelation' and the way in which God 'manifests His own Being' into history.
4. Teachings about the oneness of humankind.
5. Teachings about social issues, such as elimination of prejudices, equality of men and women, the agreement of science and religion; economic justice, and many others.
6. Teachings about personal life areas, such as marriage, burial, inheritance, abstinence from alcohol and drugs, and others.
7. Teachings about prayer, fasting, meditation and the spiritual life.

But let me end, as I always do, with several prayers. Both these prayers, as you will see, are about 'prayer.' I hope you find them as moving and interesting as I did when I first heard them.

"Intone, O My servant, the verses of God that have been received by thee, as intoned by them who have drawn nigh unto Him, that the sweetness of thy melody may kindle thine own soul, and attract the hearts of all men. Whoso reciteth, in the privacy of his chamber, the verses revealed by God, the scattering angels of the Almighty shall scatter abroad the fragrance of the words uttered by his mouth, and shall cause the heart of every righteous man to throb.

"Though he may, at first, remain unaware of its effect, yet the virtue of the grace vouchsafed unto him must needs sooner or later exercise its influence upon his soul. Thus have the mysteries of the Revelation of God been decreed by virtue of the Will of Him Who is the Source of power and wisdom." Bahá'u'lláh, *Gleanings*, 1939, 295)

And another prayer, about the subject of prayer, but from 'Abdu'l-Bahá, the son of Bahá'u'lláh:

"Make firm our steps, O Lord, in Thy path and strengthen Thou our hearts in Thine obedience. Turn our faces toward the beauty of Thy oneness, and gladden our bosoms with the signs of Thy divine unity. Adorn our bodies with the robe of Thy bounty, and remove from our eyes the veil of sinfulness, and give us the chalice of Thy grace; that the essence of all beings may sing Thy praise before the vision of Thy grandeur.

"Reveal then Thyself, O Lord, by Thy merciful utterance and the mystery of Thy divine being, that the holy ecstasy of prayer may fill our souls - a prayer that shall rise above words and letters and transcend the murmur of syllables and sounds - that all things may be merged into nothingness before the revelation of Thy splendor.

"Lord! These are servants that have remained fast and firm in Thy Covenant and Thy Testament, that have held fast unto the cord of constancy in Thy Cause and clung unto the hem of the robe of Thy grandeur. Assist them, O Lord, with Thy grace, confirm with Thy power and strengthen their loins in obedience to Thee.

"Thou art the Pardoner, the Gracious." ('Abdu'l-Bahá: *Bahá'í Prayers*, 70-71)

If you would like to learn more about the history of the Bahá'í Faith or the teachings of Bahá'u'lláh, read *Questions from Christians: About Bahá'u'lláh and the Bahá'í Faith*, from which these two chapters were taken. Another chapter from that same book discusses similarities and differences between the Christian and Bahá'í Faiths. You can order that book from amazon.com. Also, other books recently written can be ordered from amazon.com. They are: *Vanderbilt Boys... and what about the Girl?* (the story of the Declaration of Faith of Bill Hatcher, Lucia Graham Sims and Thom Thompson in 1957); *Every Good Thing: Bahá'í Scriptures Chosen for the Christian Believer* and this book: *Famous Christians: In Bahá'í History*.

Another good source for learning about the Bahá'í Faith would be to go to: bahai.org where there is a wealth of information.

CHAPTER 3

Why this book was Written

QUESTION: I'm looking at the table of contents and not sure I understand the structure of the book. What kind of book is it?

RESPONSE: There are several different kinds of books, or genres. This book is simply a personally chosen list of those Christians who are famous in my estimation for reasons that I will explain several paragraphs down. It might even be referred to as 'personally selected stories,' as suggested by one reader. Don't look for a 'structure.' There isn't one. It is a list and nothing more. Equally, don't look for the book to follow some logical path (other than the simple one that will be explained later). Looking for some 'method,' other than the making of a personally chosen list would be fruitless. Finally, don't look for it to be chronological. 'List books,' like this one, tend to organize themselves into categories, so one cannot think along a chronological line.

Just remember: It is only a list. I hope you enjoy reading about the very unusual persons in my list.

QUESTION: Why are you writing this book?

RESPONSE: That's the same question you asked me when I started my book: *Questions from Christians: About Bahá'u'lláh and the Bahá'í Faith.* Don't you have any new opening lines? And before you ask, this book will also be written in 'conversational' form. I'm in my fortieth year as a college professor and dialogue just has a better 'fit' for me. I hope you appreciate it, too.

QUESTION: I do like the format, but please answer my question. Why this book, and why now? I understood your last book. You said you were from a Christian background, experienced salvation in Christ when you were fifteen and that you were studying at Vanderbilt University Graduate School of Divinity, to become a Christian minister, when you declared your faith in Bahá'u'lláh as Christ Returned. And, you said that you wanted to write about Bahá'u'lláh and the Bahá'í Faith in a way that Christians would best understand.

RESPONSE: Well, I'm glad you remember my rationale. Yes, my Faith in Christ meant everything to me. When I heard Bahá'u'lláh say **"If ye be intent on crucifying once again Jesus, the Spirit of God, put Me to death, for He hath once more, in My person, been made manifest unto you,"** (Bahá'u'lláh, *Gleanings, 1939,* 100) this was a very clear claim that the Christ to whom I gave my life at age sixteen, had returned to the world. I knew I would have to find the truth of that claim, one way or the other. Obviously, what I discovered, and as I understood it, Bahá'u'lláh was the Return of Christ in the Glory of the Father.

QUESTION: Wait a minute. That's a little over the top, isn't it? Bahá'u'lláh associating Himself with 'the Father'?

RESPONSE: It would be better if I don't go 'off track' and begin repeating what is spelled out in *Questions from Christians*, but in that book, it is clearly stated that Bahá'u'lláh claimed to be **"the Father of all mankind."**

QUESTION: Yes, now I remember. And, it's coming back to me that you quoted Bahá'u'lláh, when He said to all Christians: **"Tell Me then: Do the sons** [that is, the Christians] *recognize the Father, and acknowledge Him, or do they deny Him, even as the people aforetime denied Him (Jesus)?"* (Bahá'u'lláh, *Proclamation of Bahá'u'lláh*, 1978, 97)

But, listen, you still haven't answered my question. Why this book? Are you telling me that Christians played roles in Bahá'í history? Since the Bahá'í Faith began in Iran, a Muslim country, I wouldn't have thought there would be that many Christians around. And, wouldn't they have been a persecuted sect?

RESPONSE: Why this book? Well, over the years, I was as shocked as you seem to be that there were many Christians who played a part, sometimes a very important part in the Bahá'í story. Yes, the Bahá'í Faith started in Persia, modern Iran, which was a Muslim country.

However, Christians often forget that in the Qur'án, Christians are recognized as 'people of the Book'[7], and Muhammad expressed tolerance toward Christians, which existed in all Muslim lands until modern times. Today however, anger and mistrust on both sides,

---

7 Based on the Qur'án, Muslims even believe that Jesus will return at the 'time of the end.' In addition, the Qur'án has quite a bit more material on the Virgin Mary than has the Bible.

Islam and Christianity, have made it difficult for Christians to live and worship in Iran and some other Muslim countries. (And, I might add, because of intolerance and ignorance, it has been, at times and in some places difficult for Muslims to live in the United States and the western world in general.)

QUESTION: So, were there that many Christians in the time of Bahá'u'lláh?

RESPONSE: Remember, we are talking about the 1800's. The years of Bahá'u'lláh's birth and ascension are 1817 - 1892. In those years, there were small Christian communities and even Presbyterian missionaries in major cities in Iran.

QUESTION: I started to argue with you about the use of the word 'ascension,' but then I remembered what you said in *Questions from Christians*, that it is the Spirit of Baha'u'llah, that ascended to the Divine Being that manifested Him. I'm going to have to go back and re-read that. But, there were missionaries in Iran!? And why Presbyterians?

RESPONSE: There *were* missionaries, and several of them interacted with Bahá'u'lláh and His followers, as you will find out later. Presbyterians, for the following reason: While Christians were divided about many things in the nineteenth century, they agreed on one thing; they believed the message of Christ should be taken **'*into all the world,*'** as Christ had asked them to do. But, they shrewdly realized that the Christian message would be diluted and perhaps not even understood if they showed up with many different and conflicting denominations. Different denominations decided to choose areas where they would concentrate their efforts. The Presbyterians focused in on the middle-east and Iran in particular.

But, you keep leading me astray with new questions. I want to answer your original question. First, this book is offered to you because I noticed there were so many Christians in the very first century of Bahá'í history. Second, in numerous cases, these Christians played very important roles, even to the extent that one Christian saved Bahá'u'lláh's life and another Christian actually gave his life to save the life of Bahá'u'lláh.

You will hear the proof of it all as you read on. There are missionaries, Bible scholars, physicians, Army Captains, Kings and Queens, Diplomats and a host of ordinary people, all Christians, who played a role in the developing story of the Bahá'í Faith and its message of peace and unity. Some of these Christians played strong, definitive roles, and others, ordinary people, played minor but, I think, important roles.

But, before we continue though, I believe there is a need to define what I mean when I use the word 'famous.' As it turns out, this is a very 'slippery' word, which is used in so many different contexts that it can easily lose its meaning or be misapplied. Here is my examination of the several parts, but it is not an exhaustive list. I simply want to show that the word is widely used

1. Famous can refer to someone who is known for special achievement or discovery.
2. Famous can refer to someone who someone who lived an outstanding and commendable life.

3. Famous can refer to someone who did despicable, terrible things, in which case we refer to them as 'infamous.' (But notice that the word famous is still in there.) Think Hitler, Stalin or Pol Pot.
4. Famous can refer to someone widely known in a culture as a writer or poet or entertainer or sports figure.
5. Famous can refer to political leaders.

However, while some of the persons listed in this book fall into one of these groups listed above, the category that is left out of this general list is a group of persons you will see highlighted in this book - *Famous Christians.* That category is the group of people who are *not famous today*, in any of the terms listed above, but who are likely to become famous in coming centuries. What do I mean?

Let's do an experiment: Quick, think of someone famous in the first three-hundred years after the birth of Christ. I'm guessing that you came up empty or with only one or two names. If you came up with Matthew, Mark, Luke and John or St. Paul, keep in mind that the only reason you or anyone knows their name is their association with Jesus, the Manifestation of God that they followed. Had they not been Christians, we would not know their names. Remember this: They were entirely ordinary. One a tent-maker, one a hated tax collector and three others laborers who were likely illiterate. But, because of their discipleship as followers of Jesus, they became, over time, 'famous' to us.

In this same way, I am going to present a list of Christians, some of whom are famous in their own right (or infamous), but most of whom are entirely ordinary today, but who I believe will be 'Famous Christians' in coming centuries. Why? Because of their association with Baha'u'llah as a Manifestation of God. In some cases, they became followers of Baha'u'llah. In most cases, they will be famous in coming centuries simply by having being around him, by providing some service to him or in some way acting to protect his health, safety and welfare. One example, with details later. In the New Testament, there is a famous 'Woman at the Well,' who gives Jesus a drink of water and enters into a conversation with him. We don't even know her name, but she is famous.

Thousands of sermons have been preached about her.

Some of the Christians in this book are 'infamous' instead of famous because of their opposition to Baha'u'llah. There are several Moslems (I will justify their inclusion later). Several of them opposed Baha'u'llah, persecuted, tortured, imprisoned or exiled Him. One would certainly have had Him killed, had it not been for a 'famous Christian' who intervened in an effective way. As the Bahá'í Faith grows and knowledge of Bahá'u'lláh is widely known in the world, the names of these famous (and infamous) Christians will be well known. Without their positive or negative association with Baha'u'llah, they would be forgotten within several centuries, known only to scholars. Today, we know the name of Tiberius Caesar, twenty centuries later, *only* because one of the gospels mentions his name.

Likewise, hundreds of years from now we will know the name of the Ottoman Sultan ('Abdu'l-Aziz) who exiled and imprisoned Baha'u'llah, while otherwise he would be effectively forgotten. That is why he is in my list (even though he is a Moslem; I will justify this later.) Many centuries from now, when the teachings of Baha'u'llah and the story of his Coming will have permeated strongly into the entire world, we will know the name of several nineteenth century kings and a queen, but only because Baha'u'llah wrote important letters to them. Otherwise, they would fade into insignificance, known only to historians. One could not tell the full story of Baha'i history without the telling of these all-important letters to the sovereigns of the world; most of these letters were written to Christian emperors or kings (and a queen) who in addition to being the political leaders, were often also titular heads of the Christian Faith in their dominions.

So, the list of famous and a few infamous Christians below is to be understood as famous largely and sometimes entirely because of their association with Baha'u'llah, whom Baha'is believe to be a Manifestation of God and the Return of the Spirit of Christ.

QUESTION: You are getting my interest. But, you are going to have to do some work to show me that Christians played any important roles in Baha'i history, let alone some significant roles. I'll reserve my judgment on that.

RESPONSE: Fair enough. There is one more reason for writing this book. I began to feel that I had no choice but to write about the role of Christians in the Bahá'í Faith that had begun to mean so much to me. As you, know, Bahá'ís revere Christ and all the other manifestations of God including Moses, Buddha, Krishna and Muhammad (among others). I saw Bahá'u'lláh's message as a bridge from my belief in Christ to belief in all that God had done in the world, throughout the ages, not just two-thousand years ago. A Christian writer of the mid-twentieth century wrote a book entitled: '*Your God is Too Small*.'[8] I had begun to feel that the Christian world

---

8 J. B. Phillips, *Your God is too Small*. (New York: Touchstone, 2004, [1952].

needed a 'Greater God' and a 'Larger Christ.' And, I felt that the larger world needed to conceive of a 'Larger God.'

It fascinated me to find these many Christians who contributed to the story of my expanded Faith. However, the real 'kicker' that said to me: "You have to write about this" was the following: Bahá'u'lláh was persecuted throughout His life by the same two forces that persecuted and caused the crucifixion of Christ, namely, clergy and political leaders. As a result of this persecution, Bahá'u'lláh was tortured, imprisoned and finally, sent into exile, first to Baghdad, Iraq, then Constantinople (modern Istanbul), then to Adrianople (modern Edirne) and finally, to the worst prison of the Ottoman Empire, the prison-city of 'Akká, in what was then Syria (now Israel). 'Akká is very near to the Old Testament 'mountain of the Lord,' Elijah's Mt. Carmel.

House of Bahá'u'lláh with Selimiye Mosque in background, Edirne/Adrianople, Turkey.

The story I want to tell you is what happened when Bahá'u'lláh had been in Adrianople/Edirne for four years, where He had been exiled. He and His family did not know that something very frightening was about to occur. There was a sudden incident one winter morning. His house was surrounded by army troops. Let Bahá'u'lláh describe it:

Know thou, O servant, that one day, upon awakening, We found the beloved of God at the mercy of Our adversaries. Sentinels were posted at every gate and no one was permitted to enter or leave. Indeed, they perpetrated a sore injustice, for the loved ones of God and His kindred were left on the first night without food." (Bahá'u'lláh, *Summons*, 2002, 145.)

On that morning, a large and diverse crowd of people had gathered around the House and they all began to weep and wail, since the populace of Edirne had learned to love and respect Bahá'u'lláh. The crowd was more than just Bahá'ís, but included Jews, Christians, Muslims and others. They all feared for his life and they feared losing his Presence. Bahá'u'lláh tells us:

"The people surrounded the house, and Muslims and Christians wept over Us, and the voice of lamentation was upraised between earth and heaven by reason of what the hands of the oppressors had wrought. We perceived that the weeping of the people of the Son [that is, Christians] *exceeded the weeping of others -- a sign for such as ponder."* Bahá'u'lláh. *Summons*, (2002) p. 144.

Within a few days, Bahá'u'lláh was again banished to 'Akká, (in what was then Syria, but now is Israel), to spend all the years of His life in prison or under 'house arrest.'

QUESTION: People were outside the house weeping? I don't understand.

RESPONSE: Wherever Bahá'u'lláh went, in His successive banishments, he eventually won over the people of that town or place. He was seen as a beloved figure, as was Christ in the Gospel. The people of Adrianople (Edirne), not just the Bahá'ís, but Christians and Muslims, Jews and others, did not want Him to leave their midst. They recognized and felt that being near to Him was to be nearer to God.

Even if they did not have specific belief in Him as a new Manifestation of God, they saw him as a 'holy man.' They feared He would be taken away and they also feared for His life. As for the loud weeping, remember that this was a middle-eastern Muslim country (Turkey), where public expression of emotion, including public crying and wailing is commonly accepted and easily displayed.

So, when Bahá'u'lláh asks me and now asks you, to question why the Christians were weeping louder than others, and even says that this is a *"a sign for such as ponder"* I think we have a mystery on our hands. Why, indeed?

This book is my response to Bahá'u'lláh's challenge to us 'to ponder.' I believe the answer is, or at least here is my best answer as to why the Christians were weeping louder: I think that these Christians were responding to Bahá'u'lláh in a unique way. And, that Bahá'u'lláh often appealed to Christians in a special way, to follow Him to become, as He asked them to be, *"the quickeners of mankind."* [9]

---

[9] *"Come ye after Me, that We may make you to become quickeners of mankind."* Bahá'u'lláh, *The Proclamation of Baha'u'lláh*, Wilmette, IL, Bahá'í Publishing

I think this: that Christians were responding to Bahá'u'lláh so strongly, because in His voice and in His words, they heard echoes of Jesus.

You learned in my previous book *Questions from Christians*, that Bahá'u'lláh wrote a special letter to all Christians, often called: 'Letter to the Christians'. I've included that entire letter in the last chapter of this book.

As for 'famous Christians,' you are now about to find out about this important group of Christian believers who played their role in the Bahá'í story. Then, maybe you will have an answer to Bahá'u'lláh's question. Get ready to 'ponder.'

Now, if I haven't yet given you enough of an answer to why this book is being written, let me summarize. Baha'u'llah gave the people of the world a challenge, a puzzle, asking us to 'ponder,' that is to think deeply about why the Christians were responding in a more deep emotional way to the danger He was facing. He even said there was a 'sign' in this Christian response. Do you like puzzles? I do. I wanted to ponder this to find out what 'sign' I was supposed to see and I told you my finding several paragraphs above.

But after accepting this challenge from Baha'u'llah and deciding to look for the 'sign' that I might find, I then noticed for the first time how many Christians show up in the story of the beginning of the Faith of Baha'u'llah. I was fascinated about that and I still am. I'm still looking for a fuller understanding of the 'sign' Baha'u'llah wants me to find. I hope you will join me in this search.

Trust, *1978)*, 91

CHAPTER 4

Why call these Christians 'Famous'?

§

QUESTION: Well, OK, I see that there may have been Christians in Iran and Iraq and that these Christians may have interacted with Bahá'u'lláh, even helped him in some way. But, why call them 'famous'? Isn't what they did fairly ordinary and, if so, why are you paying such attention to them?

RESPONSE: Some of the acts were not 'ordinary' at all. One Christian saved Bahá'u'lláh's life and another actually gave up his life, choosing to die to save Bahá'u'lláh. Not very ordinary, although some of the Christians I will tell you about did things that were not special and not at all extraordinary. I still call them 'famous Christians' for what I believe is a very good reason.

Maybe this will help. Let's remember that Bahá'u'lláh came out of Iran (ancient Persia), and spent all His life either in Iran, Iraq or Syria (a part of Syria that is now Israel). Ninety to ninety-five per-cent of everyone in those countries were Muslim. There were Christians in these countries and even entire Christian villages and communities or Christian 'quarters' in various towns (in Iraq, for example). There were also Jews and Jewish communities in most middle-eastern countries, but in a distinct minority. It just seems to me unusual that among these few Christians in Muslim countries, there were several that played such an important part in the early history of the Bahá'í Faith.

Here is a 'fantasy analogy' that may help us. Turn on your imagination and consider this scene. We are back in the time of Jesus, in a Jewish country (Israel), but we find (this was certainly *not* the case) that there is a small minority of Buddhist monks and believers and that they talked with Jesus and on occasion helped him. Some did things that contributed to the safety and well-being of Jesus and other acts contributed in some way to the energy and dynamism of the new Christian Faith.

We further learn (this is fantasy, remember, but with a purpose) that one of these Buddhists did something to save Jesus' life. We even learn that another Buddhist gave his life; he chose to die, so that Jesus might live! And, we learn that Jesus Himself testified to the truth of this sacrifice.

Tell me this: would you not call these Buddhists 'famous' in terms of the Christian story? Wouldn't you see them as unusual and special players in the establishment of the Christian Faith?

Now, come back out of this fantasy, come to Iran and Iraq (Muslim countries) and see the Christians in those countries as similar to the few Buddhists in our 'fantasy experiment.' These Christians are indeed famous, I say, partly because most of us would not have expected to find them there, doing what they did, responding to Bahá'u'lláh's call, even to the point of risking or sacrificing their lives, so that the Bahá'í Faith might be protected and the teachings of Bahá'u'lláh could become a beacon of light and unity for the entire world.

QUESTION: All right, I see your point. These Christians were very unusual. However, It is hard for me to believe that they did such unusual things, such as you say they did. I'm reserving judgment, again. I think you had better give me an example.

RESPONSE: Sounds reasonable. May I present: Dr. Petro. Yes, that's his name. When Bahá'u'lláh was in 'Akká (in what is now northern Israel), the grim prison city used by the Ottoman Empire for their worst criminals, he was kept for years in a four-room section of an imposing stone prison. The Sultan's Edict that sent Him there specifically said that He and His family were not to have any visitors, no contact of any kind with the people in the city outside the large prison or with anyone outside of 'Akká. And, especially important, no messages in or out. No communication of any kind. The Sultan wanted them to be cut off entirely from society and there was to be no communication *of any kind* between Bahá'u'lláh, His family and followers in 'Akká and the larger community of followers in Iraq, Iran and India.

Enter Dr. Petro, a physician (probably English) who saw to the medical needs of the prisoners. He became a friend of Bahá'u'lláh and soon was smuggling messages in and out of the prison, in the lining of his hat! He also reassured the Governor of 'Akká that even though the Bahá'ís (about seventy of them, including friends and family) had been advertised as criminals and blasphemers, nevertheless, were not the dangerous criminals that they had been advertised to be. (Hmm? That line about 'criminals and blasphemers' ought to remind both you and me of the taunting of Jesus by Romans and Pharisees?)

Those messages carried in the lining of Dr. Petro's hat were the only means of reliable communication that Bahá'u'lláh or the other prisoners had for the better part of a year. Tens of thousands of followers back in Persia waited anxiously and hopefully for word from Bahá'u'lláh, to hear what they believed was the Revelation of God and to be assured that the One they followed was still alive. Thank you, Dr. Petro, for your aid to Bahá'u'lláh and for the part that you played in the Bahá'í story. [10]

QUESTION: If Bahá'u'lláh was a prisoner and the state authorities had sent Him to prison, why are we, why are you, treating Him with such reverence?

RESPONSE: Pardon me if I show a bit of upset that you don't remember a conversation we had in *Questions from Christians*. I'm sure you must remember that Jesus was executed, crucified by the state and religious authorities for 'blasphemy' and (mistakenly) for being a criminal threat to the Roman Empire.

QUESTION: Yes, OK, I do remember. Can you give me another example of what you call 'famous Christians'?

RESPONSE: Sure. Remember that scene in Edirne (Adrianople) where Bahá'u'lláh thought the Christians were weeping louder than the Jews or Muslims?

---

10 Moojan Momen. *Bahá'u'lláh*. Oxford: Oneworld, 2007), 95.

Missionaries who Aided Bahá'u'lláh

Well, there were some Christian missionaries who did more than weep. Although we don't know their names, several of them tried to talk with the authorities to prevent harm from coming to Bahá'u'lláh. When they learned of his impending banishment, they were especially alarmed and went to the foreign consuls in the town, imploring them to use their influence with their governments to persuade the Ottoman Sultan to lessen or cancel Bahá'u'lláh's punishment and banishment. I thank them and hold them as 'famous.'

While we are on the subject of Christian missionaries (who play an ongoing part in Bahá'í history, (some for good, some on the critical side) here is Rev. James Neil, an English missionary. He investigated the Bahá'í Faith extensively and interviewed Bahá'u'lláh's son, 'Abdu'l-Bahá (who is very central in the Bahá'í story). Rev. Neil said: "We had a long interview with the son of their prophet. It was indeed strange to find an Eastern in Syria [northern Israel in modern times] so well educated, and to hear him speak so tolerantly and intelligibly of Christ and Christianity…We would not but deeply sympathize with this persecuted sect."[11]

British Consul in Edirne, Turkey

There was a British Consul in Edirne, John Blunt, who testifies to the character of the prisoners (there were about seventy people in all with Bahá'u'lláh, including His family and close followers, who had chosen to go with Him into further banishment and prison). Blunt tells us that Bahá'u'lláh is "regarded with sympathy, mingled with respect and esteem" by the local community. Also, that the local

---

11 ibid, 112.

government regarded Bahá'u'lláh "with respect and consideration." Finally, Blunt tells us that the "harshness and severity" with which the order to further banish Bahá'u'lláh was carried out created "sympathy and compassion of all classes of the population." Thank you, Consul Blunt, for setting the record straight that Bahá'u'lláh and His entourage were good citizens rather than the criminals and blasphemers the Sultan of the Ottoman Empire portrayed them to be.[12]

Representative of the British Government

Prior to being sent to 'Akká, and even prior to being in Edirne, Bahá'u'lláh had been banished from His native land of Persia (Iran) to Iraq. While there, the Consul-General in Iraq, representing Queen Victoria, entered into friendly correspondence with Bahá'u'lláh and several times, visited Him. He realized that Bahá'u'lláh was in danger of further banishment. This representative, Colonel Sir Arnold Kemball offered Him the protection of the British Crown. Col. Kemball even offered to transfer Bahá'u'lláh to India or to any other place in the vast British Empire. Though thankful for this help, Bahá'u'lláh declined and chose to remain in Ottoman Empire territory. Thank you, Consul-General Kemball. I'm happy to add you to the group of 'famous Christians' in the Bahá'í story.[13]

Foreign Consuls in Edirne

The Sultan of the Ottoman Empire had consular relations with many European countries, so those countries, including France and Great Britain had similar consulates, such as those that were in Edirne, at the time of the incident we have described. Several of these consuls

---

12 Ibid, 84
13 Shoghi Effendi. *God Passes By*. (Wilmette, IL: Bahá'í Publishing Trust, 1944), 131

went to Bahá'u'lláh, offering aid and assistance. (Alas, they are nameless.) To them, Bahá'u'lláh said: [these are not Bahá'u'lláh's actual words, but the words remembered by one of His followers] "You wish me to give you the word to bring Me relief, but My relief lies in the hands of God. My focus is God, and to Him alone do I turn." (as remembered by a follower named Ashchi of Kashan, cited in H. M. Balyuzi's great book: *Bahá'u'lláh: The King of Glory.*[14])

In a Tablet written by Bahá'u'lláh, He refers again to these consular officials who spontaneously offered help: "**The consuls of that city** [Edirne, Turkey] **gathered in the presence of this Youth at the hour of His departure and expressed their desire to aid Him. They, verily, evinced toward Us manifest affection.**" [15]

OTHER MISSIONARIES IN THE BAHÁ'Í STORY

There is the story of a pompous man, a missionary, Reverend Doctor Robert Bruce, of Britain, who was traveling in Iran and asked for an interview with a famous scholar and Bahá'í teacher - Mirzá Abu'l Fadl. Dr. Bruce seemed to want to do most of the talking, much of which consisted in bragging about his good works and his conversion of a very small number of Muslims to the Christian Faith. We must remember that Muslims already believe in Christ and His divine mission. For a Muslim to convert to Christianity would be, in their view, to take a step backward, to reduce belief, rather than to enlarge it. Thus, we can understand the lack of success of Christian missionaries in Muslim lands.

---

14 H. M. Balyuzi. *Bahá'u'lláh, the King of Glory.* Oxford: George Ronald, 1980), 256

15 Shoghi Effendi. *God Passes By.* (Wilmette, IL: Bahá'í Publishing Trust, 1944), 180

Finally, after hearing at length from Dr. Bruce, Mirzá Abu'l Fadl realized that the missionary felt that after many years of work put in, that he believed only two of the thirty converts would be able to remain true to their new Faith. Mirzá Abu'l Fadl said this to the good doctor: "If you will permit me, I will now recount my position for you. Financially, I have no assets whatsoever. At times, I even have nothing to subsist on…Should people suspect that I am a Bahá'í they would undoubtedly put me to death in public [There was terrible persecution of the followers of the Báb, and later, followers of Bahá'u'lláh in Iran]. …as to my knowledge, it is true that I have learnt religious subjects as are currently taught in Islamic schools. I am, nevertheless, born in and a product of a society steeped in ignorance and enveloped in darkness.

"In spite of all my shortcomings, I have spoken to about one hundred people since my arrival in this city [Isfahan, Iran] a month ago. Twenty four souls among them have recognized the truth of this Faith [the Bahá'í Faith] and embraced it with such devotion and fervour that every one of them is ready to lay down his life in the path of God, as many other Bahá'ís have already done. Now, I want to ask you to be fair in your judgement. Who, in this day, is assisted by the Holy Spirit, you or I?" Those present said that the missionary became very uncomfortable and asked for an end to the meeting.[16]

AN ANGRY MISSIONARY: There are quite a few missionaries in the Bahá'í story, some of them helpful and interested in the Faith, but some others who were angry and perhaps jealous of the success

---

16 Adid Taherzadeh. *The Revelation of Bahá'ulláh*. (Oxford, George Ronald, 1987 (Vol. 4), 263-6

of the Bahá'ís in contrast to how little they had been able to accomplish over several generations of effort. One of these was William McAlwee Miller, (NOT the William Miller of millennial fame, to be discussed later) who went to Iran in the 1930's, stayed for thirty years, then spent literally the rest of his long life writing and speaking against the Bahá'í Faith. I've often wondered what it must be like to look back on a life of opposition, a life totally dedicated to being 'against' something. But, this was Rev. Miller's 'passion.' I guess I can give him an 'E' for effort, or something but he is, nevertheless, an '(in)famous' Christian' in the Bahá'í story.[17]

QUESTION: Who is the person you spoke of a moment ago called 'the Báb'?

RESPONSE: The Báb (His name means 'Gate,' was the forerunner of Bahá'u'lláh, just as John the Baptist was the forerunner of Jesus. Bahá'u'lláh tells us He was a Manifestation of the 'Word of God,' which is why I have capitalized His pronoun. You can learn more about Him by consulting the first two chapters of this book. Chapter One tells the history of the beginning of the Bahá'í Faith. Chapter Two tells about Bahá'u'lláh's teachings. I'll tell you now that while there are, of course, some differences between Bahá'í and Christian teachings, the similarities are strong and may surprise you. There is a chapter in my former book, *Questions from Christians: About Bahá'u'lláh and the Bahá'í Faith* with the title:

---

17 Details on Miller can be found in wikipedia.com Also, see: Martin, Douglas (1978). *"Missionary as Historian: William Miller and the Baha'i Faith, a review of Miller's 'The Baha'i Faith: Its History and Teachings."* Baha'i Studies **40** (3).

'Similarities and Differences between the Christian and Bahá'í Faiths.'[18]

Another Missionary Brings the Bahá'í Faith to America

QUESTION: Surely you don't mean he taught the Bahá'í Faith?

RESPONSE: No, but he *was* the first person to mention the Bahá'í Faith in North America. It was at the 'Columbian Exposition' in Chicago, 1893, commemorating Columbus's famous discovery of a so-called 'New World.' (Well, every time I hear the phrase 'New World,' I try to remember that it was new to Europeans, but hardly new to the millions of Native Americans, who had lived there for over ten thousand years.)

But, anyway, this man who first mentioned the Bahá'í Faith in the United States, Dr. Henry Harris Jessup, was another Presbyterian missionary who was familiar with the Bahá'í Faith and apparently had some sympathy toward it and, as a result, played his role in Bahá'í history. (Rev. Jessup did not actually attend the World Parliament of Religions that was held in conjunction with the Chicago World's Fair, but a paper written by him was read by a Rev. Ford.) Referencing the Ascension of Bahá'u'lláh the year before (1892), he said: "…just outside the Fortress of 'Akká, on the Syrian coast, there died a few months since, a famous Persian sage, the Bahá'í saint, named Bahá'u'lláh – the 'Glory of God' – the head of that vast reform party of Persian Muslims, who accept the New

---

18 Order a kindle or paperback from amazon.com

Testament as the Word of God and Christ as the Deliverer of men, who regard all nations as one, and all men as brothers."

He went on to quote the only westerner who ever interviewed Bahá'u'lláh, the scholar and Professor E. G. Browne (we shall hear more from him later) in a truly memorable quote: Browne says he heard this from Bahá'u'lláh: ***"Let not a man glory in this, that he loves his country; let him rather glory in this, that he loves his kind."*** We will pick up on the rest of the quote from Dr. Browne later. Rev. Jessup also said that the words "gave utterance to sentiments so noble, so Christ like."

Dr. Henry Harris Jessup

Rev. Jessup helped found Syrian Protestant College, now known as the University of Beirut. He was highly thought of and though offered, he turned down the post of Secretary of the Presbyterian Missionary Board, Professorship at Union Theological Seminary and the office of United States Minister to Persia. I think Rev. Jessup deserves to be in the 'famous Christian' category, by virtue of his being the first to speak publicly the name of Bahá'u'lláh to the American public, an act unprompted and spontaneous.[19]

QUESTION: Well, so far all you have produced are some people weeping, some missionaries, some British representatives and a doctor who smuggled messages out of a prison. This doesn't really qualify as 'famous' for me.

RESPONSE: Remember that these 'famous Christians' were not necessarily famous in their own right, but famous they still are in the sense that Christ's disciples Matthew, Mark, Luke and John are famous to us, even though in their day no-one would have even seen them even as special, and certainly not famous. And, as for Dr. Petro, he risked imprisonment, perhaps even his life, by smuggling out those messages. The Sultan, in imprisoning Baha'u'llah, expressed in writing that there was to be 'no communication' coming out or in of the prison. This meant that without the valiant effort of Dr. Petro, the thousands of followers of Baha'u'llah in Iran and Iraq (and other places, such as India) would not have had contact with him for many months; they would not even have known that he was alive.

---

19 Bahá'í World, Vol. 2. Wilmette, IL: Bahá'í Publishing Trust, 1928), 169.

But, all-right, how about a Canon of the Episcopal Church, an internationally famous Biblical Scholar, and just to season the mix, let's throw in a Queen and a King. Also, we'll tell you about five other Christians who were among the earliest followers of Bahá'u'lláh. One of them was a minister. And, one was the first citizen of the United States to declare belief in Bahá'u'lláh. He was also the first person and first Christian of the 'western world' to become a Bahá'í.

CHAPTER 5

A Canon of the Church, A Biblical Scholar, a Queen… and a King (all of whom became Bahá'ís.)

§

CANON OF THE CHURCH: Rev. George Townshend (1876-1957) was an Irish priest who rose to the level of Archdeacon of Clonfert, then to Canon of St. Patrick's Cathedral in Dublin. Earlier, he had gained fame as a writer of many books, among them: *Altar on the Hearth* and *The Genius of Ireland.*

As a young man, he travelled to the United States and taught English at the University of the South, in Sewanee, Tennessee, returning to Ireland and to the priesthood. From an earlier time, he had learned about the Bahá'í Faith and began a correspondence with 'Abdu'l-Bahá, the son of Bahá'u'lláh. He studied the faith throughout his life and finally, shortly after becoming the Canon of St. Patrick's, declared his faith in Bahá'u'lláh. When he declared, and after resigning from the priesthood, he wrote a letter entitled: *The Old Churches and the New World Faith.* It was distributed by the National Spiritual Assembly of Great Britain to over eight thousand persons, including the British and Irish clergy, the House of Commons, leaders of thought, heads of universities and colleges and many others.

Rev. George Townshend, Canon of St. Patrick's Cathedral, Dublin

He then wrote several books on the Bahá'í Faith, including *Heart of the Gospel; The Mission of Bahá'u'lláh; Christ and Bahá'u'lláh* and my favorite, his paean to Bahá'u'lláh, *The Promise of all Ages.* Late in his life, he was appointed as a 'Hand of the Cause,' by Shoghi Effendi, Head of the Bahá'í Faith in the first half of the twentieth century. (1922 – 1957, prior to the establishment of the Universal House of Justice in 1963.) Keep in mind that the Bahá'í Faith does not have a clergy. Here is a poem from Townshend's pen about Baha'u'llah that I think is revealing of Townshend's mystical depth.

Only Beloved! With a heart on fire
And all my longings set in one desire
To make my soul a many-stringed lyre
For Thy dear hand to play,
I bend beneath Thy mercy-seat and pray
That in the strength of perfect love I may
Tread with firm feet the red and mystic way
Whereto my hopes aspire.

I have forgotten all for love of Thee
And ask no other joy from destiny
Than to be rapt within Thy unity
And - whatso'er befall –
To hear no voice on earth but Thy sweet call,
To walk among Thy people as Thy thrall
And see Thy beauty breathing throughout all
Eternal ecstasy.

Lead me forth, Lord, amid the world's ways,
To bear to Thee my witness and to raise
The dawn song of the breaking day of days.
Make my whole life one flame
Of sacrificial deeds that shall proclaim
The new-born glory of Thy ancient name;
And let my death lift higher yet the same
Triumphal chant of praise![20]

---

[20] This poem is found in: George Townshend. *The Mission of Bahá'u'lláh and other Literary Pieces.* (Oxford: G. Ronald, 1952), p. 121. For more on the life of Townshend, see his biography: *George Townshend* by David Hofman, George Ronald, 1983.

BIBLICAL SCHOLAR: The best known and internationally recognized Bible scholar of the late 1800's, early 1900's was Rev. Dr. Thomas Kelly Cheyne, or T. K. Cheyne (1841-1915). An Englishman, a Professor of Theology at Oxford, a Fellow of the British Academy, he dedicated his life to Biblical study and what was called, at the time, Higher Criticism. He wrote numerous books and articles and was best known for being the co-editor of a monumental and famed four-volume reference work, the Encyclopedia Biblica.[21]

He became a follower of Bahá'u'lláh in the early years of the twentieth century. At a time when Bahá'u'lláh's son, 'Abdu'l-Bahá visited England in 1912, Dr. Cheyne was the first person to greet him when he stepped off the boat. 'Abdu'l-Bahá gave him a new name, Ruhani (Spiritual) which Cheyne used as a signature and 'Abdu'l-Bahá also referred to the scholar as "my spiritual philosopher." He also said: "It is...my hope that in the future the East and West may become conscious that thou wert a divine philosopher and a "herald of the Kingdom."[22] We don't know the circumstances of how T.K. Cheyne learned of the Baha'i Faith, but we can make an educated guess that one of the English ladies, possibly Lady Blomfield, who had visited 'Abdu'l-Baha informed him of the appearance of a new Revelation from God.

In his book, the Reconciliation of Races and Religions, Rev. Cheyne said of Bahá'u'lláh: "There was living quite lately a human being of such consummate excellence that many think it permissible

---

21 A description of Cheyne's life and work can be found in any encyclopedia, including online at Wikipedia.
22 Found in the preface, no pagination, of: T. K. Cheyne. *The Reconciliation of Races and Religions* (London, A and C Black, 1914).

and inevitable even to identify him mystically with the invisible Godhead."[23] "If there has been any Prophet in recent times," asserts the Rev. T. K. Cheyne in his book, 'The Reconciliation of Races and Religions', "it is to Bahá'u'lláh that we must go. Character is the final judge. Bahá'u'lláh was a man of the highest class - that of Prophets."[24]

Dr. Thomas Kelly Cheyne

Another statement by Dr. Cheyne: "The want of a surely attested life, or extract from a life, of a God-man will be more and more acutely felt. [Author's Note: Dr. Cheyne refers to modern times in this next sentence] There is only one such life; it is that of Bahá'u'lláh.

---

23 Ibid, 2
24 ibid, 71

Through Him, therefore, let us pray in this twentieth century amidst the manifold difficulties which beset our social and political reconstructions; let Him be the prince-angel who conveys our petitions to the Most High."[25]

Thank you, Rev. Dr. T. K. Cheyne, for being a 'herald of the Kingdom.' To me, as a prominent Biblical scholar who became a follower of Bahá'u'lláh, you are a 'famous Christian.'

Queen Marie of Romania

Queen Marie of Romania

---

25 ibid, 111

Queen Marie, originally a member of the British Royal family, became the consort of King Ferdinand I of Romania and during the 1930's said this about the Bahá'í Faith:

"Their writings," she states: "are a great cry toward peace, reaching beyond all limits of frontiers, above all dissension about rites and dogmas…the Bahá'í teachings bring peace to the soul and hope to the heart. To those in search of assurance the words of the Father are as a fountain in the desert after long wandering.

"It is like a wide embrace, gathering together all those who have searched for words of hope. It accepts all great Prophets gone before, ' it destroys no other creeds and leaves all doors open…. The Bahá'í teaching … is Christ's Message taken up anew…. If ever the name of Bahá'u'lláh or `Abdu'l-Bahá comes to your attention, do not put their writings from you. Search out their books, and let their glorious, peace -bringing, love-creating words and lessons sink into your hearts as they have into mine."[26]

And a King!

The King of Western Samoa, His Highness Susuga Malietoa Tanumafili II, declared his faith in Bahá'u'lláh in 1973. He was the first reigning sovereign to become a Bahá'í. (Queen Marie declared her belief in Bahá'u'lláh after her husband ascended the throne, and though she was the Queen and royalty, she herself was not the sovereign.) On the passing of the Malietoa at age ninety-four, in 2007, at which time he was the world's longest reigning monarch, the international governing body of the Bahá'ís, the Universal House of Justice wrote:

---

26 Bahá'í World, Vol. 8, 1941

"His service to the people of Samoa as Head of State was distinguished by the high principles, genuine compassion and personal humility that characterized the constancy of his concern for the welfare of all. As the first reigning sovereign to accept the Message of Bahá'u'lláh, he set a record that will forever illumine the annals of our Faith, one that future generations will increasingly extol. His great interest for well-nigh four decades in the Faith's progress was reflected in the enthusiastic affirmation of his belief whenever the opportunity presented itself and in the abiding joy with which he regarded the construction in 1984 of the Mother Temple of the Pacific Islands in Samoa...."[27] The independent state of Samoa was blessed with the construction of one of the Bahá'í Houses of Worship in its capital city of Apia, in 1984.

Five Christians who Became Bahá'ís

There were very many more than these five Christians who decided, early in the history of the Faith, to follow Bahá'u'lláh, but here are five who stand out.

FARIS EFFENDI: It is believed that Farris Effendi was the *very first* Christian to become a Bahá'í, which certainly gives him fame. This was in the late 1860's. We will tell you more about his story later, but for now, let me say he was a physician and was in prison in Alexandria, Egypt, when taught the Faith by a fellow prisoner who was a Bahá'í. He is additionally famous because he wrote a letter to Bahá'u'lláh announcing his Declaration of Faith and received a reply from Bahá'u'lláh. More later, including excerpts from Faris Effendi's

---

27 See Bahá'í World News Service, Bahá'í International Community, 14 May 2007.

letter, when we tell you about Constantine the Watchmaker, the Christian who delivered Faris' letter to his newly found Lord.[28]

'Abdullah Túzih: There was a Christian 'quarter' in the prison city of 'Akká, and one of the Christians there became an strong supporter of the Bahá'ís and later, an enthusiastic follower of Bahá'u'lláh and a teacher of the Faith. It was difficult to be a supporter at that time and even more difficult to pledge your life to Bahá'u'lláh. The people of 'Akká had been told (mistakenly) that the Bahá'ís were blasphemers and criminals. We have no further knowledge of Abdullah, but this very early declaration of Faith, when it was not easy to become a Bahá'í, is enough to make him a 'famous Christian' for me.[29]

Reverend Howard Colby Ives: Reverend Ives was a Unitarian minister who encountered 'Abdu'l-Bahá, when the son of Bahá'u'lláh travelled in the United States in 1912. Reverend Ives had founded his own church called the 'Brotherhood Church.' After meeting with 'Abdu'l-Bahá several times, Ives invited him to speak in his church.

Because of the name of the church, 'Abdu'l-Bahá chose to speak on 'The Brotherhood of Mankind.' After the service, Ives and the Master met in an adjoining room ('Abdu'l-Bahá was often referred to as 'the Master' by the Bahá'ís. It is a common term used in the middle-east for a holy person or a person of great knowledge.)

Sitting together with the Master, both of them remained silent, until 'Abdu'l-Bahá waved the interpreter out of the room ('Abdu'l-Bahá

---

28 Adib Taherzadeh, *The Revelation of Bahá'u'lláh*. (Oxford, George Ronald, 1983, Vol. III), 5-11
29 Ibid. 13.

spoke little English, since his native language was Persian (Farsi). He also knew Arabic and some Turkish. But then, when the Master spoke to Reverend Ives, he used English, telling Ives that he was 'my dear son.' The minister broke into a flood of tears because he realized that he did in fact have a belief that Bahá'u'lláh was the new Manifestation of God.

In another conversation, the Master told Ives "with great emphasis: 'This is a Day for Very Great Things.' Three times he repeated this, looking at me with such intentness and meaning. 'Remember, Mr. Ives, what I say, this is a Day for Very GREAT Things.'" Within a short time, Ives left the ministry and dedicated the rest of his life to spreading the news of Bahá'u'lláh as Christ Returned.

Late in his life, in 1936, he wrote what is now a famous book entitled *Portals to Freedom* detailing his entire spiritual journey toward becoming a follower of Bahá'u'lláh. A fascinating book, it can be ordered from amazon.com or from Bahá'í Distribution Service.[30] Another Unitarian minister who wrote about the Faith, Rev. Alfred Martin, said this: "Who shall say but that just as the little company of the Mayflower, landing on Plymouth Rock, proved to be the small beginning of a mighty nation, the ideal germ of a democracy which, if true to its principles, shall yet overspread the habitable globe, so the little company of Bahá'ís exiled from their Persian home may yet prove to be the small beginning of the world-wide movement, the ideal germ of democracy in religion, the Universal Church of Mankind?" [31]

---

30 Also, see the internet site: Bahá'í Heroes and Heroines, December 13, 2009
31 See bahaitributes.wordpress.com

Stanwood Cobb: Mr. Stanwood Cobb did not hold a doctorate, but was called Dr. Cobb by everyone, high and low, as a term of respect and because he held high positions in the educational field that led people to assume higher educational credentials. He founded and was director of the well-respected Chevy Chase Country Day School, a private school in Chevy Chase, Maryland (a Washington, DC suburb) attended by children of diplomats from around the world. He also had a home and a summer camp for children in Eliot, Maine, near the Green Acre Bahá'í summer school.

Stanwood Cobb

Valedictorian at Dartmouth, he then studied at Harvard Divinity School, thinking that he would be a Unitarian minister. Hearing a talk by Thornton Chase, the first American Bahá'í, he soon became a follower of Bahá'u'lláh. He taught at the United States Naval Academy and overseas at Robert College in Turkey. He wrote two books (among twenty-five others) about his experience in Turkey, namely, *The Real Turk* and *Islamic Contributions to Civilization* (this one is available on line).[32] Other, more comprehensive books on this subject have now been written, but Cobb was early, and among the first, to point out the many gifts to Western Civilization that came through Islam.[33]

Becoming interested in 'progressive education,' he helped found the Association for the Advancement of Progressive Education, becoming its first president (famed Philosopher John Dewey was the second president). Dr. Cobb lived nearly to one-hundred-one ('Abdu'l-Bahá had assured Cobb he would live to be one-hundred) and wrote his autobiography in the several years before his death in 1982. That autobiography was called: *A Saga of Two Centuries.*

Cobb had met 'Abdu'l-Bahá, the son of Bahá'u'lláh, on five occasions, both in 'Akká and again in Europe and the United States, when 'Abdu'l-Bahá traveled to the Europe and America. He later became a leader in Bahá'í affairs in the United States, speaking and writing, contributing to the early journal *Star of the West* and becoming the first editor of the Bahá'í periodical *World Order.*

---

32 Stanwood Cobb wrote a great deal of poetry and even wrote a romantic novel called *Ayesha of the Bosphorus*, which some suspect to be autobiographical. It can be found on the internet and is an interesting read.

33 Cobb detailed dozens of contributions of Islam, among them preserving the learning of Plato and Aristotle during the so-called 'Dark Ages' of Europe and a little thing, for example, called '*al-jabr*' (algebra); Muhammad ibn Mūsā al-Khwārizmī (c. 780–850) was responsible for establishing the discipline of modern algebra. Contributions were in areas of mathematics, astronomy, physics, medicine, literature, art, music and technology. For a quick introduction to these many contributions, see article in Wikipedia on: 'Islamic Contributions to Medieval Europe.' Also, I think you may be able to find Cobb's book online.

[Author's Note: My path toward becoming a Bahá'í was started after reading Cobb's book *Security in a Failing World*. I feel exceptionally privileged to have known him personally for decades and to have had his advice and tutelage as a mentor.][34]

Thornton Chase

Thornton Chase: (1847-1912) I cannot do this strikingly unusual person justice in this small space. See the footnote below for a place to read more of his remarkable, creative life. In the Civil War he was second in command of 100 men of the Twenty-Sixth United States Colored Troops (Chase was Caucasian). Wounded by cannon, he was later promoted to Captain, with his own company.

---

34 Though Wikipedia can change constantly, in this instance it is an excellent source for information on Cobb, including a list of all twenty-seven of his books.

With an early life described by him as 'loveless and lonely,' (mother died when he was an infant, so he tells us he had "neither mother, brother or sister") he suffered many sad experiences, though he coped by learning to sing and act. In 1894, his life changed greatly when he became a Bahá'í. He developed as an active follower of Bahá'u'lláh, making a pilgrimage to the Holy Land in 1907 to see 'Abdu'l-Bahá. Later, he wrote a book about the pilgrimage, entitled *In Galilee*. Another book followed: *The Bahá'í Revelation*. He wrote poetry and among many other accomplishments, he helped found the Bahá'í Publishing Board and held many leadership positions in the Faith.

He is a 'famous Christian' for many reasons, including being the first person and first Christian in the United States to become a Bahá'í. In addition, he is the first person from the 'Western World' to become a Bahá'í[35]

QUESTION: OK, now I'm more interested and left wondering why I haven't heard these things before, or why many people haven't heard about the Bahá'í Faith, for that matter. Why is that?

REPONSE: Usually (not always) religions grow slowly. After several decades, Islam grew very quickly, while Christianity had the usual slow early growth and many people in the Roman Empire would not have heard about it until three hundred to four hundred years after Christ, so it's not strange at all that you wouldn't have heard about the Bahá'í Faith, because it is only halfway through its second century. (If Roman citizens in the third and early fourth century did

---

35 For information on James Brown Thornton Chase, see: bahai-encyclopedia-project.org. Chase was listed as the first 'steadfast' Bahá'í in "the West," and he is known as the first American believer.

hear about Christianity they would have regarded it as a small Jewish cult or as an atheistic cult, since Christians refused to give worship to Roman Gods).

There are probably not more than six to seven million Bahá'ís in the world, as of the early twenty-first century, so the news of the arrival of Bahá'u'lláh as 'the Father of all mankind' has not yet strongly penetrated into the thought and attention of the larger body of the world. However, the Encyclopedia Britannica does state that the Bahá'í Faith is, next to Christianity, the most widespread faith on the planet.

There is a saying that while there are not many Bahá'ís anywhere, there are some Bahá'ís everywhere. Let's go on in the next chapter to some other interesting people who I say are 'famous Christians' in the Bahá'í story.

CHAPTER 6

More Kings, and another Queen, and a President of the United States

QUESTION: There were more kings and queens that became Bahá'ís? And a United States President. Surely not!

RESPONSE: No, I separated this President and these Kings and this Queen from the others, because even although they did not become followers of Bahá'u'lláh, they nevertheless played an important part in the Bahá'í story.

When Bahá'u'lláh was in Adrianople (modern Edirne), beginning in 1867, He began to write epistles, or letters to important sovereigns in the Western and Middle Eastern World. He continued His 'Summons to the Kings' after his eventual and final banishment to 'Akká, across the bay from Mt. Carmel, the 'mountain of the Lord,' which then was part of Syria, now Israel. He wrote Nasiri'd-Din Shah of Persia/Iran, as well as the Sultan 'Abdu'l-Aziz, of the Ottoman Empire. Napoleon III, Tsar Alexander II of Russia, Pope Pius IX (yes, He wrote a letter to the Pope; more on this later), and finally, He wrote to Queen Victoria of England. In addition though He did not write directly to Kaiser Wilhelm I, Emperor Franz Joseph and the Rulers of the Americas, he addressed them in the book – Kitáb-i-Aqdas.

And the tablets or letters addressed to the above, Bahá'u'lláh tells us that they all were finally received. The messages to Kaiser Wilhelm, Franz Joseph and the Rulers of the Americas cannot be proven to be received, but the Bahá'ís of the time were very ardent and efficient, so one can speculate that these messages were also delivered, though there is no proof. In later years however, these messages were then made known to the leaders or governments of all of them, such as Rulers of the Americas.

Regarding that message He addressed to the 'Rulers of the Americas,' this would have included President Grant. Even if we speculated (with no convincing proof) that this message was ever delivered, there is no definitive word if Grant or his government ever saw this important message. One wonders if this document did somehow arrive and lays gathering dust in our National Archives. When Bahá'u'lláh's son, 'Abdu'l-Bahá traveled to the United States in 1912 he offered this prayer:

"O Thou kind Lord! This gathering is turning to Thee. These hearts are radiant with Thy love. These minds and spirits are exhilarated by the message of Thy glad tidings. O God! Let this American democracy become glorious in spiritual degrees even as it has aspired to material degrees, and render this just government victorious. Confirm this revered nation to upraise the standard of the oneness of humanity, to promulgate the Most Great Peace, to become thereby most glorious and praiseworthy among all the nations of the world. O God! This American nation is worthy of Thy favors and is deserving of Thy mercy. Make it precious and near to Thee through Thy bounty and bestowal." ('Abdu'l-Bahá, *The Promulgation of Universal Peace*, 1982, 67)

If you are wondering why Bahá'u'lláh addressed these rulers and sovereigns, this can be best described by quoting from an internet page called: *Summons to the Kings*. "Beginning in September, 1867, Bahá'u'lláh wrote a series of letters to the world leaders of his time…In these letters, Bahá'u'lláh openly proclaimed His station. He spoke of the dawn of a new age. But first, He warned, there would be catastrophic upheavals in the world's political and social order. To smooth humanity's transition, He urged the world's leaders to pursue justice. He called for general efforts at disarmament and urged the world's rulers to band together into some form of commonwealth of nations. Only by acting collectively against war, He said, could a lasting peace be established."[36]

Bahá'u'lláh's Letter to Queen Victoria

Queen Victoria of Great Britain

---

36 Get more information at: www.bahaullah.com/bahaullah-summons or at: http://reference.bahai.org/en/t/b/SLH/slh-3.html.

QUESTION: Wait a minute. I'd like to know if these letters were ever received? Also, how can we know they were read?

RESPONSE: Bahá'u'lláh Himself says that they were all received (save for one; see below under the section on Tsar Alexander II). We can be reasonably certain that they were read, at least in several instances. The letter to Queen Victoria seems to have been read by her, because (although there is no reliable proof of this) she is reputed to have said: "If this is of God, it will endure; if not, it can do no harm." [37]

This reminded me, and I suspect you too, of the Jewish Pharisee Doctor of Law and teacher of the Apostle Paul - Gamaliel - who was consulted about what to do with early apostles of Jesus who had been arrested and brought to the high council of the Sanhedrin, for a decision on their fate. He said [Acts.5:38-9]: "…if this plan or undertaking [i.e. Christianity] is of human origin, it will fail; but if it is of God, you will not be able to overthrow them – in that case you may even be found to be fighting against God."

Good for you, Queen Victoria. You are in good company, with one of the great Jewish scholars! Interestingly, Bahá'u'lláh praised the Queen for halting the slave trade and for the development of a democratic state, with a parliament.

---

[37] Many Bahá'í authors say "it is reported that" Queen Victoria said this. For example, Hand of the Cause William Sears in his book *The Prisoner and the Kings*, Ch. 7 says: According to one written account: "Queen Victoria, it is said, upon reading the Tablet (Letter) revealed for her, remarked: *'If this is of God, it will endure…'*" For full quote, see Shoghi Effendi, *The Promised Day is Come*. (Wilmette, IL: Bahá'í Publishing Trust), *66*.

In the letter, Bahá'u'lláh states: ***"O Queen in London! Incline thine ear unto the voice of thy Lord, the Lord of all Mankind…cast away all that is on earth, and attire the head of thy kingdom with the crown of the remembrance of thy Lord, the All-Glorious. He, in truth, hath come unto the world in His most great glory, and all that hath been mentioned in the Gospel hath been fulfilled."*** (Bahá'u'lláh, *Summons*, 2002, 88.)

Here are other passages from the letter to Queen Victoria. In the first two passages, Bahá'u'lláh praises Queen Victoria for banning the slave trade and for establishing representative democracy. ***"We have been informed that thou hast forbidden trading in slaves, both men and women. This, verily, is what God hath enjoined in this wondrous Revelation. God hath, truly, destined a reward for thee because of this."*** (ibid. 88)

While we cannot know the nature of the 'reward' that Bahá'u'lláh promises to the Queen, we should remember that He also promised a 'special station' to Tsar Alexander for the help rendered to Him by the Russian government. Here's my thought: Their reward (or 'station') may be the fact that both of them shared a granddaughter, Queen Marie of Romania, who was brought to belief in Bahá'u'lláh several generations later. Bahá'u'lláh continues to speak to Queen Victoria, interestingly placing strong approval on a form of democracy and putting forth one of the earliest voices calling for debt-control and disarmament.

"We have also heard that thou hast entrusted the reins of counsel into the hands of the representatives of the people. Thou, indeed, hast done well, for thereby the foundations of the edifice of thine

affairs will be strengthened, and the hearts of all that are beneath thy shadow, whether high or low, will be tranquillized.

"It behoveth them, however, to be trustworthy among His servants, and to regard themselves as the representatives of all that dwell on earth. " (ibid. 173)

O kings of the earth! We see you increasing every year your expenditures, and laying the burden thereof on your subjects. This, verily, is wholly and grossly unjust.... lay not excessive burdens on your peoples. Do not rob them to rear palaces for yourselves; nay rather choose for them that which ye choose for yourselves... Your people are your treasures... By them ye rule, by their means ye subsist, by their aid ye conquer. Yet, how disdainfully ye look upon them! How strange, how very strange! (ibid. 93)

"Take ye counsel together, and let your concern be only for that which profiteth mankind and bettereth the condition thereof.... (ibid. 90)

[In the next passage, Bahá'u'lláh introduces a key Bahá'í teaching, which is the principle of 'collective security.'] *"Be united, O concourse of the sovereigns of the world, for thereby will the tempest of discord be stilled amongst you and your peoples find rest. Should any one among you take up arms against another, rise ye all against him, for this is naught but manifest justice."* (ibid. 95)

Bahá'u'lláh tells us that the world is like the human body, originally *"whole and perfect"* but now afflicted with *"grave ills."* He then gives God's Plan for 'the healing of the world': **That which the Lord** *hath ordained as the sovereign remedy and mightiest instrument for the healing of all the world is the union of all its peoples in one universal Cause, one common Faith. This can in no wise be achieved except through the power of a skilled, an all-powerful and inspired Physician."* (ibid. 91)

Within the message to Queen Victoria, Bahá'u'lláh includes a prayer for her to use. Here is a part of that prayer: *"Turn thou unto God and say: O my Sovereign Lord! I am but a vassal of Thine, and Thou art, in truth, the King of Kings. I have lifted my suppliant hands unto the heaven of Thy grace and Thy bounties. Send down, then, upon me from the clouds of Thy generosity that which will rid me of all save Thee, and draw me nigh unto Thyself... Assist me, then, O my God, to remember Thee... and to aid Thy Cause in Thy lands. Accept, then, that which hath escaped me when the light of Thy countenance shone forth. Thou, indeed, hast power over all things. Glory be to Thee, O Thou in Whose hand is the kingdom of the heavens and of the earth."* (ibid. 95) [38]

Bahá'u'lláh's Letter to Czar Alexander II of Russia

Here is what Bahá'u'lláh said about the delivery of all of His Tablets to the rulers of the western world, but in particular, this letter: The following several sentences are not the actual words of Bahá'u'lláh, but are the reported words of Bahá'u'lláh, as heard by Nabil, historian and writer of the book *Dawnbreakers*. "The rest of the Epistles [letters to kings and queens] likewise <u>reached their destination</u> [underlining by author]...The epistle We addressed to the Czar of

---

38 See bahaiteachings.org/Bahaullah-addresses-queen-victoria for an excellent article with pictures of the Queen, both as a young woman and older.

Russia, alone failed to reach its destination. Other tablets however, have reached him, and that Epistle will eventually be delivered into his hands." (Nabil: Dawnbreakers, 1932, 586)

Its delivery was attempted by an embassy official who was favorable to the Bahá'í Faith. In the letter to the Czar, Bahá'u'lláh said: *"O Czar of Russia! Incline thine ear unto the voice of God, the King, the Holy, and turn thou unto Paradise…"* And: *"Whilst I lay chained and fettered in the prison* [His imprisonment in 1853 in Teheran], *one of thy ministers extended Me his Aid. Wherefore hath God ordained for thee a station which the knowledge of none can comprehend except His knowledge. Beware lest thou barter away this sublime station."* (Bahá'u'lláh: *Summons*, 2002, 56)

Later, we are going to hear more about that 'minister' of the Czar who helped Bahá'u'lláh (actually, probably saved His life, as it turns out). We've already heard that Queen Marie, who became a follower of Bahá'u'lláh, was descended from both the Czar and Queen Victoria. This may explain Bahá'u'lláh's reference to a 'special station' for the Tsar. Other passages from the letter to Tsar Alexander:

Bahá'u'lláh says the most striking thing to the Czar, telling him that He had overheard the prayer of the Czar (but put your own interpretation on this): *"We, verily, have heard the thing for which thou didst supplicate thy Lord, whilst secretly communing with Him. Wherefore, the breeze of my loving-kindness wafted forth, and the sea of My mercy surged, and we answered thee in Truth. Thy Lord, verily, is the All-Knowing, the All-Wise."* (ibid. 82)

As in letters to other Kings and Queens, Bahá'u'lláh lets the Czar know in no uncertain fashion Who He is, and that the Czar is hearing from the 'King of Kings': ***"Beware lest thy sovereignty withhold thee from Him Who is the Supreme Sovereign. He, verily, is come with His Kingdom, and all the atoms cry aloud: 'Lo! The Lord is come in His great majesty!' He Who is the Father is come, and the Son,*** [i.e., Jesus] ***in the holy vale, crieth out: 'Here am I, here am I, O Lord, My God'..."*** (ibid. 89)

QUESTION: I have to break in on you here. Isn't Jesus the 'King of Kings'? And why is Bahá'u'lláh saying He is 'the Father'?

REPONSE: Jesus, and all the other manifestations, Bahá'u'lláh tells us, fill the role of 'King of Kings,' since they all are the 'Word of God'[39] to the age in which they appear. If you read these 'Tablets' in their entirety (I hope you will), you will certainly see that the tone of these letters is that of a sovereign talking to subjects. Bahá'u'lláh said many times (see below in the His letter to Pope Pius IX) that ***"Lo! The Father is come, and that which ye were promised in the Kingdom is fulfilled!"*** (Bahá'u'lláh, quoted in: Shoghi Effendi, *The Promised Day is Come*, 1980, 52).

---

[39] Rev. Barbara Berry-Bailey, one of the 'beta' readers of this book comments that "many mainline denominations understand the 'Word of God' as a three-strand cord that cannot be separated – the written word, the preached word and Jesus, the Word made flesh. Therefore, an ordained minister's sermon or interpretation of the scripture is considered to be the Word of God, as well as what is written in the Bible." This is my understanding also, as a former minister of Christ. The Bahá'í view connects with the third part of that 'strand,' the part where Bahá'u'lláh is the 'human Temple' (Bahá'u'lláh's words) in which the Presence of God or 'Word of God' can be experienced. Of course, Bahá'u'lláh's entire Revelation is considered by Bahá'ís to be 'the Word of God.'

More from the letter to the Czar; just in case the Czar missed the point, Bahá'u'lláh tells him: *"I am the one Whom the tongue of Isaiah hath extolled, the One Whose name both the Torah and the Evangel* [the Old and New Testaments] *were adorned."* (Bahá'u'lláh, *Summons*, 2002, 85)

Finally, just as Bahá'u'lláh had offered to Queen Victoria a prayer that she could pray, he tells the Czar that when he has heard the words that are in this letter, he can pray to God as follows: *"Praise be to Thee, O Lord of all the worlds, inasmuch as Thou hast made mention of me through the tongue of Him Who is the Manifestation of Thy Self at a time when He was confined in the Most Great Prison* ['Akká], *that the whole world might attain unto true liberty."* (ibid. 88)

Bahá'u'lláh warns the Czar and all mighty rulers (in words so similar to those used by Jesus): *"O proud ones of the earth! Do ye believe yourselves to be abiding in palaces whilst He Who is the King of Revelation resideth in the most desolate of abodes? Nay, by My life! In tombs do ye dwell, could ye but perceive it. Verily, he who faileth, in these days, to be stirred by the breeze of God is accounted among the dead in the sight of Him Who is the Lord of all names and attributes. Arise, then, from the tombs of self and desire and turn unto the Kingdom of God, the Possessor of the Throne on high and of earth below, that ye may behold that which ye were promised aforetime by your Lord, the All-Knowing.*

"Think ye that the things ye possess shall profit you? Soon others will possess them and ye will return unto the dust with none to help or succour you. What advantage is there in a life that can be overtaken by death, or in an existence that is doomed to extinction, or in

a prosperity that is subject to change? Cast away the things that ye possess and set your faces toward the favours of God which have been sent down in this wondrous Name." (Bahá'u'lláh, *Summons*, 87)[40]

Bahá'u'lláh's Two Letters to Napoleon III of France

This sovereign received two letters. The first was sent from Edirne, (prior to 1868) the second letter was sent from 'Akká, *before* Napoleon's defeat in 1870).[41] Napoleon III, the French Emperor received his letter, we know, because it was delivered by a 'famous Christian' and also because Napoleon was reputed to have given a shameful response.

Napoleon III of France

---

40 Wikipedia gives an excellent review of the Czar's life and accomplishments; among those accomplishments was the freeing of the serfs of Russia. He told the nobles at one point that it was better that a movement to free the serfs begin at the top instead of at the bottom. Judging by what happened a generation later, that freedom was not fully effective.

41 This defeat soon after Bahá'u'lláh's prediction of Divine Justice lead some people to accept the Bahá'í Faith, since it seemed to them as fulfilment of prophecy.

A well-known student of the East, the Comte de Gobineau, who had been the ambassador of the French court to the Shah of Persia, had also been in correspondence with Bahá'u'lláh. He personally carried the letter to Napoleon. (Author's Note: We probably need to call Gobineau an 'infamous Christian,' however, since he is widely acknowledged as the intellectual father of modern racism, someone whose views were quickly accepted later by Nazism. Sadly, his views were widely shared by many average Christians of the time, in the nineteenth century, including most Europeans and United States citizens).

The contents of this letter were to apprize the King of the condition of the prisoners in Edirne, where they were unjustly held under effective banishment and sometimes, house arrest. Bahá'u'lláh tells Napoleon III:

"Two statements graciously uttered by the king of the age have reached the ears of these wronged ones. These pronouncements are, in truth, the king of all pronouncements, the like of which have never been heard from any sovereign. The first was the answer given the Russian Government when it inquired why the war (Crimean) was waged against it. Thou didst reply: 'The cry of the oppressed who, without guilt or blame, were drowned in the Black Sea wakened me at dawn. Wherefore, I took up arms against thee.' These oppressed ones, [the family and followers of Bahá'u'lláh] *however, have suffered a greater wrong, and are in greater distress. Whereas the trials inflicted upon those people lasted but one day, the troubles borne by these servants have continued for twenty and five years, every moment of which has held for us a grievous affliction.*

"The other weighty statement, which was indeed a wondrous statement manifested to the world, was this: "Ours is the responsibility to avenge the oppressed and succour the helpless." ***The fame of the Emperor's justice and fairness hath brought hope to a great many souls. It beseemeth the king of the age to inquire into the condition of such as have been wronged, and it behooveth him to extend his care to the weak. Verily, there hath not been, nor is there now, on earth any one as oppressed as we are, or as helpless as these wanderers."*** (Bahá'u'lláh, quoted in Shoghi Effendi, *The Promised Day Is Come*, 1980, 51-2)

Bahá'u'lláh 'tone' in this letter is modest, unlike His second letter to Napoleon, where He is majestic and commanding in tone. He is complimenting the King for his empathy and his perceived justice toward the weak and powerless and requesting him to look into the intolerable situation of His family and followers whom he named the 'wronged ones.' We should remember that they had endured twenty five years of suffering including being cast out from their native land of Persia. They had been severely persecuted from the mid-1840's in Persia, and then banished successively from Iran to Baghdad, then to Istanbul, finally to Edirne, in Turkey.

Very shortly after the writing of this letter, they were sent on a final banishment, to 'Akká, the Ottoman Empire 'prison city.' At many times during these years, they were in the greatest deprivation. Their treatment, Bahá'u'lláh tells the King, was supremely unjust. The letter was soft in tone and certainly conciliatory and was requesting Napoleon as 'the King of the Age' to look into the treatment of the Persian exiles. However, Napoleon's response was insulting and degrading. Napoleon, having heard the letter, is reputed to have cast it on the ground and stepped on it, declaring: "If this man is God, I am two Gods."[42] There is no record of these actual words, but they are reported and Bahá'u'lláh Himself refers to Napoleon III, *"who is reported to have made a certain statement, as a result of which We sent him Our Tablet while in Adrianople. To this, however, he did not reply..."* Bahá'u'lláh here seems to be referring to Napoleon's insulting remark

When you read the second letter to Napoleon III, you will understand why the King was not inclined to reply. Bahá'u'lláh also says in the second epistle to Napoleon that he shows his insincerity by having **"cast behind thy back"** the first letter He had sent to the King (see below). The evidence seems heavily in favor of the anecdote that says that Napoleon threw the first letter on the floor, stepped on it and said: "If this man is God, I am two Gods." (But, I stress, this is not certain; however, having read a little about this King, it fits what is known about his outlook and personality.)

A Christian Translated the Second Letter to Napoleon III

Bahá'u'lláh wrote a second letter which was translated from Arabic into French by famous Christian Louis Catafago, the French Consular agent in 'Akká. He also transmitted this second letter. The letter was smuggled out of the prison in a man's hat (not the hat of Dr. Petro, already mentioned, which leads me to think the security detail in these prisons were really missing the need to search hats, since this is the second episode of 'hat skullduggery.')

---

42 See Shoghi Effendi. *The Promised Day is Come.* (Wilmette, IL: Bahá'í Publishing Trust, 1961), *51.*

By the way, Catafago's son, Cesar Ketaphakou, after reading this letter and after seeing Bahá'u'lláh's prophecy of Napoleon's downfall vindicated, became a follower of Bahá'u'lláh, another 'famous Christian.' [43] Probably because of Napoleon's duplicity and disdain, Bahá'u'lláh had stated in the second letter that Napoleon's Kingdom would be taken from him (which it was just a couple of years later -1870- at the battle of Sedan).

Bahá'u'lláh's actual words were: *"For what thou hast done, thy kingdom shall be thrown into confusion, and thine empire shall pass from thine hands, as a punishment for that which thou hast wrought. Then wilt thou know how thou hast plainly erred. Commotions shall seize all the people in the land, unless thou ariseth to help this cause, and followest Him Who is the Spirit of God* [44] *in this, the* **Straight Path**...*we see abasement hastening after thee, whilst thou art of the heedless."* (Bahá'u'lláh, *Summons*, 2002, 71-2). These remarkable words of prophecy of Napoleon's downfall were uttered by Bahá'u'lláh at the height of Napoleon's power.

QUESTION: Why did Bahá'u'lláh refer to Himself, as the Spirit of God? You told me He usually uses 'the Spirit of God' to refer to Jesus. Here, He seems to refer to Himself.

RESPONSE: Don't forget that Bahá'u'lláh said: *"If ye be intent on crucifying once again Jesus, the Spirit of God, put Me to death, for*

---

43 'Abdu'l-Bahá, *Some Answered Questions*, (Wilmette, IL: Bahá'í Publishing Trust, 1964), 33.
44 Bahá'ulláh almost always uses 'the Spirit of God' to refer to Christ; here, however, he refers to Himself. But remember, as quoted before, He said to us that Jesus was again presented to us **"in My person."**

He hath once more, in My person, been made manifest unto you." Bahá'u'lláh, *Gleanings*, 1939, 100) So, Bahá'u'lláh definitely felt that in calling the King to follow 'this Cause,' He was not only calling him to follow Himself, but Christ, as well.

There are other very interesting and striking passages in this second letter to Napoleon III, including the way it begins: *"O King of Paris! Tell the priests to ring the bells no longer. By God, the True One! The Most Mighty Bell hath appeared in the form of Him Who is the Most Great Name,* [that is, Bahá'u'lláh] *and the fingers of the will of Thy Lord, the Most Exalted, the Most High, toll it out in the heaven of Immortality, in His name, the All-Glorious."* (Bahá'u'lláh: *Summons*, 2002, p 67)

He continues, with a statement that signifies His Mission: *"Say: He Who is the Unconditioned is come, in the clouds of light, that He may quicken all created things with the breezes of His Name, the Most Merciful, and unify the world, and gather all men around this Table which hath been sent down from heaven."* (ibid. 131) Bahá'u'lláh several times in this tablet, even though He chastises and punishes Napoleon III for his previous behavior, still exhorts him to 'arise' to serve God and help His cause. He makes an astonishing statement to the king: *"Arise thou to serve God and help His Cause. He, verily, will assist thee with the hosts of the seen and unseen, and will set thee king over all that whereon the sun riseth. Thy Lord, in truth, is the All-Powerful, the Almighty."* (ibid., p. 69)

The letter to Napoleon III contains many of Bahá'u'lláh's most striking writings and teachings, such as: *"He Who is your Lord, the*

All-Merciful, cherisheth in His heart the desire of beholding the entire human race as one soul and one body. Haste ye to win your share of God's good grace and mercy in this Day that eclipseth all other created Days" (Bahá'u'lláh: *Summons*, 2002, 81) and *"Know of a truth that your subjects are God's trust amongst you. Watch ye, therefore, over them as ye watch over your own selves. Beware that ye allow not wolves to become the shepherds of the fold, or pride and conceit to deter you from turning unto the poor and the desolate."* (Bahá'u'lláh: *Summons*, 2002, 75)

Finally, Bahá'u'lláh tells Napoleon that he has been 'tested' and 'found wanting' as to his sincerity and says: *"Hadst thou been sincere in thy words, thou wouldst have not cast behind thy back the Book of God, when it was sent unto thee by Him Who is the Almighty, the All-Wise."* (ibid. 75) [45]

---

[45] Biography.com does an excellent presentation on Napoleon III. Fun fact: Famous actress Sarah Bernhardt performed for Napoleon III. She also wanted to write and perform the story of the life of an early Bahá'í heroine named Tahirih, who was one of the disciples of the Báb. Look up Tahirih if you want to learn about the earliest spiritual birth of the modern women's movement. Tahirih's last words before being martyred by strangulation were: "You may kill me as soon as you wish, but you cannot stop the emancipation of women." Use your imagination to wonder how this sentence could have been uttered in the 1850's by a woman in the middle-east. Now, a riddle: The famous Seneca Falls Convention (New York) of 1848 is quite close in time to Tahirih's leadership role in the Bábí Faith and her own women's rights related martyrdom. This was the first meeting in the United States of women seeking their full civil rights. There was only one man at that convention and he played a big part. Who was he? None other than Frederick Douglas, who insisted that they ask for something that they had *not* planned to ask for: The Vote!

President Ullyses Grant

QUESTION: You are saying that President Grant of the United States received a message from Bahá'u'lláh?

RESPONSE: This one is a bit tricky and one reader of this manuscript considered it 'a stretch' to believe that a message was directed to Grant. I don't agree. We know that Bahá'u'lláh wrote a section in His 'Most Holy Book' addressed to the "Rulers of America and the Presidents of the republics therein." This would have included President Grant. While there is no knowledge or proof for whether or not actual messages were delivered, it seems to me unlikely that followers of Bahá'u'lláh, who were thorough and quite dedicated in their efforts, would have failed to attempt to deliver this important message to President Grant. All of the letters delivered to sovereigns or world leaders were either delivered or sent by post. So, there is no record and no evidence, but I am personally convinced that attempts would have been made to deliver this message to all the 'Presidents of the republics therein.'

At any rate, what Bahá'u'lláh said in this message to President Grant and other presidents of the American republics was this: *"Hearken ye, O Rulers of America and the Presidents of the Republics therein… Adorn ye the temple of dominion with the ornament of justice and of the fear of God, and its head with the crown of the remembrance of your Lord, the Creator of the heavens. Thus counselleth you He Who is the Dayspring of Names, as bidden by Him Who is the All-Knowing, the All-Wise. The Promised One hath appeared in this glorified Station, whereat all beings, both seen and unseen, have rejoiced. Take ye advantage of the Day of God…Give ear unto that*

which hath been raised from the Dayspring of Grandeur…Bind ye the broken with the hands of justice, and crush the oppressor who flourisheth with the rod of the commandments of your Lord, the Ordainer, the All-Wise." (Bahá'u'lláh, *Kitáb-i-Aqdas* (Most Holy Book), 1992, 52).

Before we go further, let's review all the rulers and kings that Bahá'u'lláh addressed with messages, starting in the late 1860's and continuing in later decades. They are: Pope Pius IX; Emperor Napoleon III of France; Czar Alexander II of Russia; King Wilhelm I of Prussia; Queen Victoria of Great Britain; Emperor Franz Joseph of Austria-Hungary; Sultan 'Abdu'l-"l-'Azíz of the Ottoman Empire; Násiri'd-Dín Sháh of the Persian Empire and Rulers of America (meaning all of South and North America) and the Presidents of the republics therein.

Two of the above were Muslims. The rest are 'famous Christians,' since they received messages from Bahá'u'lláh. We've already looked at the tablets to Queen Victoria, to Czar Alexander and the two tablets to Napoleon III. We are not going to quote liberally from all of these letters, but let's go on to the next chapter where we will look briefly at statements made to German Emperor Kaiser Wilhelm and Emperor Franz Joseph of Austria. Also, we will look at letters to Sultan 'Abdu'l-Aziz, leader of the powerful and far-flung Ottoman Empire; Nasiri'd-Din Shah, the King of Persia (Iran) and of special interest, the letter to Pope Pius IX. (I know several of these are not Christian and will explain later why I'm including them.)

CHAPTER 7

Still more Kings, and a Pope! And a Governor

§

KAISER WILHELM I OF GERMANY

KAISER WILHELM I, THE GERMAN Emperor, did not receive a special Tablet from Bahá'u'lláh but was addressed by Bahá'u'lláh in the book called 'The Most Holy Book,' (in Arabic, the Kitáb-i-Aqdas) the central scripture of the Bahá'í Faith. *"Say: O King of Berlin! Give ear unto the Voice calling from this manifest Temple: Verily, there is none other God but Me, the Everlasting, the Peerless, the Ancient of Days. Take heed lest pride debar thee from recognizing the Dayspring of Divine Revelation, lest earthly desires shut thee out, as by a veil, from the Lord of the Throne above and of the earth below. Thus counselleth thee the Pen of the Most High. He, verily, is the Most Gracious, the All-Bountiful. Do thou remember the one whose power transcended thy power,* [Napoleon III] *and whose station excelled thy station. Where is he? Whither are gone the things he possessed?*

"Take warning, and be not of them that are fast asleep. He it was who cast the Tablet of God behind him, when We made known unto him what the hosts of tyranny had caused Us to suffer. Wherefore, disgrace assailed him from all sides, and he went down to dust in great loss. Think deeply, O King, concerning him, and concerning

them who, like unto thee, have conquered cities and ruled over men. The All-Merciful brought them down from their palaces to their graves. Be warned, be of them who reflect." (Taherzadeh: *The Revelation of Bahá'u'lláh*, v.3, 1983, 148.)

Bahá'u'lláh then utters a divine prophecy that is chilling and remarkable in its accuracy. It is difficult for many not to see a reference to Germany's involvement in both WW I and II: **"O banks of the Rhine! We have seen you covered with gore, inasmuch as the swords of retribution were drawn against you; and you shall have another turn. And We hear the lamentations of Berlin, though she be today in conspicuous glory."** [1]

(Bahá'u'lláh, Kitáb-*i-Aqdas*, 1992, 15) [46]

Emperor Franz Joseph of Austria

Franz Joseph also did not receive a Tablet from Bahá'u'lláh but was addressed in Bahá'u'lláh's 'Most Holy Book.' This is the short paragraph referring to Franz Joseph. Before you read it, you need to know that Bahá'u'lláh had heard that the Emperor had travelled to Jerusalem to visit the well-known Aqsa Mosque, located on the Temple Mount. You will see that Bahá'u'lláh chides him for being so close to an opportunity to behold Him **"Who is the Object of this Remembrance...** [In other words, the King is visiting Jerusalem and the special 'Remembrance' of God's earlier Presence in the world [that is, Jesus], and ignoring the living Manifestation of God – Bahá'u'lláh – Who is 'the Object of this Remembrance'

---

46 Wikipedia.org seems to have the most complete information on the Kaiser, with many illustrations and pictures, but be careful to select Kaiser Wilhelm I instead of Wilhelm II.

and who is less than a day's journey from Jerusalem]. Here is the quote:

O Emperor of Austria! He Who is the Dayspring of God's Light dwelt in the prison of 'Akká at the time when thou didst set forth to visit the Aqsa Mosque. Thou passed Him by, and inquired not about Him by Whom every house is exalted and every lofty gate unlocked. We, verily, made it a place whereunto the world should turn, that they might remember Me, and yet thou hast rejected Him Who is the Object of this remembrance, when He appeared with the Kingdom of God, thy Lord and the Lord of the worlds. We have been with thee at all times, and found thee clinging unto the Branch and heedless of the Root. Thy Lord, verily, is a witness unto what I say.

"*We grieved to see thee circle round Our Name, whilst unaware of Us, though We were before thy face. Open thine eyes, that thou mayest behold this glorious Vision, and recognize Him Whom thou invokest in the daytime and in the night season, and gaze on the Light that shineth above this luminous Horizon.*" (Bahá'u'lláh, *Kitáb-i-Aqdas*, 1992, 50) [47]

[Author's Note: OK, OK, I know this book is about 'Famous Christians' in the Bahá'í Story, but, will you permit me to sneak in two Muslims? There is a reason, which is, that since we are discussing the famous Christian kings and a queen that Bahá'u'lláh addressed, it seems uneven not to include the two kings (well, one

---

47 Again, Wikipedia.org has an excellent, very complete article on Franz Joseph, with many pictures.

King/Shah and one Sultan), the sovereigns who ordered the torture, banishment and imprisonment of Bahá'u'lláh.]

Sultan 'Abdu'l-Aziz of the Ottoman Empire

From the 14th century to the beginning of the 19th century, the Ottoman Empire was far-flung and powerful, at different times controlling or influencing most of the middle-east and parts of eastern Europe. 'Abdu'l-Aziz ruled from 1861 through 1876, so his Sultanate was in power in the period during which Bahá'u'lláh was exiled from Iraq to Constantinople (Istanbul), from Constantinople to Adrianople (Edirne) and finally, the further and concluding exile to 'Akká.

It was by order of the Sultan that Bahá'u'lláh's later exiles occurred, so we can remember when we read portions of Bahá'u'lláh's letter to the Sultan that these exiles, with all their pain and suffering, their cruelty and injustice were the work of 'Abdu'l-Aziz's administration. As we will see, Bahá'u'lláh held him responsible.

Bahá'u'lláh was critical of the Sultan and his ministers for his injustices and stated several times that the Sultan should be more personally aware of the conditions of the people of his realm. ***"Seize thou, and hold firmly within the grasp of thy might, the reins of the affairs of thy people and examine in person whatever pertaineth unto them. Let nothing escape thee, for therein lieth the highest good."*** (Bahá'u'lláh, *Summons*, 2002, 211)

And, ***"Take heed that thou resign not the reins of the affairs of thy state into the hands of others...beware that thou allow not the wolf*** *to become the shepherd of God's flock, and surrender not the fate of His loved ones to the mercy of the malicious."* (ibid. 210)

Bahá'u'lláh tells the Sultan, and this is a theme of all the other letters, to *"Fear the sighs of the poor and the upright of heart who, at every break of day, bewail their plight, and be unto them a benignant sovereign…inquire into their affairs, and ascertain, every year, nay every month, their condition, and be not of them that are careless of their duty."* (ibid. 213)

The dishonesty and treachery of the Sultan's ministers is condemned and the sufferings of the exiles is made clear to the Sultan: *"The tribulations we have sustained are such that any pen that recounteth them cannot but be overwhelmed with anguish…so great have been our sufferings that even the eyes of Our enemies have wept over Us, and beyond them those of every discerning person."* (ibid. 219)

It appears the patience and forbearance of Bahá'u'lláh was wearing thin. He had frequently pointed out that He and his family and band of followers were loyal subjects and had done no wrong. When the Sultan, for the third time and for no good reason, again banished the exiles and sent them to 'Akká, this pronouncement came from Bahá'u'lláh: *"The day is approaching when the Land of Mystery* [Adrianople/Edirne] *and what is beside it shall be changed, and shall pass out of the hands of the King…by reason of that which hath befallen these captives at the hands of oppression."* (ibid. 142)

When the letter to the Sultan was being read by his Grand Vizir, we are told that he "blanched while reading the communication addressed to his Imperial master and his ministers, and made the following comment: 'It is as if the king of kings were issuing his behest to his humblest vassal king, and regulating his conduct'." [48]

As with other prophecies made by Bahá'u'lláh, in just a few years, Adrianople fell in a war with Russia and was occupied in cruel circumstances.

Ironically, when Bahá'u'lláh was in route to 'Akká, he asked an army Major named Umar to take a message to the Sultan. The message was a request for a ten minute meeting with the Sultan *"...so that he may demand whatsoever he deemeth as a sufficient testimony and regardeth as proof of the veracity of Him Who is the Truth. Should God enable him to produce it, let him, then, release these wronged ones, and leave them to themselves."* (ibid. 171) Of course, no answer was received. This was quite an opportunity for the Sultan, it seems to me, to ask for or demand something amazing or miraculous from Bahá'u'lláh and the Sultan passed it up. Oh well. He not only passed on this opportunity but on the chance to meet with 'the Father of all Mankind.' I would say this was the worst day the Sultan ever had (other than the day someone was sent to strangle him.) [49]

---

48 Shoghi Effendi. *The Promised Day is Come*. (Wilmette, IL: Bahá'í Publishing Trust, 1961), 65.
49 Go to: bahai-library.com/varqa_prophecy_supply_curve. This site will not only tell you about the Sultan. The article, *The Prophecy of Bahá'u'lláh*, will also give you detail about Bahá'u'lláh's prophecies and the fulfillment of those prophecies concerning *all* the rulers addressed by Bahá'u'lláh.

QUESTION: I am amazed that Bahá'u'lláh would refer to Himself as *'the Truth.'* Should I wonder about the mental condition of Bahá'u'lláh?

RESPONSE: Jesus was once speaking to His disciples and said: *"I am the way and the truth and the life."* If you had been present when Jesus was speaking, were of a Jewish background and had overheard this from Him, would you have thought Jesus to be crazy? Bahá'u'lláh tells us that each time a Manifestation of God appears in human history, they are the Presence of God, and therefore, *'the Truth'* against which all other truth should be measured.

Numerous writers and theologians have spoken of a 'trilemma.' Among them, C. S. Lewis and J. B. Phillips, who was fond of saying that when we listen to Jesus we have only three choices: To see Him as a madman, or a charlatan, or the only other choice is to see Him as *Who He says He is*. Other Christian apologists have said it differently. For example, John McDowell, an evangelical writer spoke in his book, *Evidence which demands a Verdict* (Thomas Nelson, 1992) of the choice being 'lunatic, liar or Lord.' C. S. Lewis pointed out that if this test is to be applied to Christ, then it must also be applied to others who claim to be the Voice of God. Those who encountered Jesus had to make up their minds and now those who encounter Bahá'u'lláh, Who claims to be the Return of the Spirit of Christ, also have a decision to make.

I guess we have the same choice about the identity of Bahá'u'lláh, as with Jesus or any other Manifestation of God. Make your choice; I have made mine with both Jesus *and* Bahá'u'lláh.

QUESTION: Well, as long as I have already interrupted you, here's another question that has been dogging me: Why, really, is Bahá'u'lláh writing to the rulers and kings? Jesus did nothing like this. His work was with the common people. What did Bahá'u'lláh hope to accomplish with these letters?

RESPONSE: Before I respond directly, we need to note that Bahá'u'lláh for years and decades before writing these letters, *did* interact with the common people. He taught among them, revealed prayers and teachings, answered questions and interpreted scripture. These letters to the kings were written in the late 1860's and during the 1870's, nearly twenty years after the start of His ministry.

What did Bahá'u'lláh want to accomplish? He speaks clearly and unmistakably that he felt these leaders could respond to Him as a Manifestation of God and to His teachings that represented the Word of God. And He states again and again that they needed to take specific actions toward building a united world and bringing mankind into a peaceful era. And, finally, that he was giving them the means and the pathway toward this goal.

Bahá'u'lláh's mission and message was tied up centrally with the need for humanity to respond to God's command to construct unity and find peace. He said His teachings would guide the way to these goals. He further stated many times that the kings of the earth were piling up armaments and heading toward conflict. One of His key teachings was that these kings and sovereigns should agree to meet and form some kind of world government that would stop the growing armament race and provide the beginning steps toward the establishment of peace.

Other teachings about the ending of human slavery, the need for international government and the idea of 'collective security, the establishment of democracy, the equality of men and women and, especially, the recognition of the oneness of the human race, among many others, were given to these leaders in these 'Letters to the Kings and the Queen.'

And, we should note that many times in history, (with Islam as an exception) a religion does not grow to any large size until someone of sovereign stature endorses that religion and its teachings (as in the case of Christianity, with Constantine). Reading these letters reminds me that Bahá'u'lláh called upon the kings to 'arise' and offered the opportunity and hoped that one or more of these decision makers would step forth proactively to provide the leadership that would be needed to make the move toward world unification and peace.[50]

A powerful example in history of this expectation of Bahá'u'lláh is Emperor Constantine's decision in C. E. 312 to institute measures favoring establishment of Christianity in the Holy Roman Empire. His decisions had great effect not only on the sudden and speedy growth of the Christian Church, but on the stability and character of the entire empire.

Christianity had experienced slow but steady growth before this, but Constantine's approval, while it did not make it the 'state religion,' did generate explosive growth for Christianity; as a result, Christian teachings began to exert a constructive influence in the Roman

---

50 Bahá'u'lláh, *Gleanings*, 207. (*"We cherish the hope that one of the kings of the earth will, for the sake of God, arise for the triumph of this wronged, this oppressed people."*)

Empire. Bahá'u'lláh was evidently giving these leaders of mankind the opportunity to do what Constantine did. Though they did not respond, the Bahá'í message then went out into the entire world. Now, people of all nations and of all social levels are responding.

The twentieth-century leader of the Bahá'í Faith, Shoghi Effendi, gave this summary as to why Bahá'u'lláh wrote to these political leaders and what his message to them was: "In these passages He (1) called upon them to take fast hold of the "Most Great Law"; (2) proclaimed Himself to be "the King of Kings" and "the Desire of all Nations"; (3) declared them to be His "vassals" and "emblems of His sovereignty"; (4) disclaimed any intention of laying hands on their kingdoms; (5) bade them forsake their palaces, and hasten to gain admittance into His Kingdom; (6) extolled the king who would arise to aid His Cause as "the very eye of mankind"; and finally (7) arraigned them for the things which had befallen Him at their hands." Bahá'u'lláh, *God Passes By*, 1944, 205)

THE SHAH OF PERSIA: [See the author's note above as to why we are including two Muslims in this story.] Bahá'u'lláh begins his letter to the Shah (King) of Persia (Iran) with a statement I cannot resist quoting because it puts me in mind of something Jesus said. Here is what Bahá'u'lláh says to the Shah: ***"Whensoever the clouds of tribulation have rained down the darts of affliction in the path of God, the Lord of all names, I have hastened to meet them, as every fair-minded and discerning soul shall attest. How many the nights which found the beasts of the field resting in their lairs, and the birds of the air lying in their nests, while this Youth languished in chains and fetters with none to aid or succour Him!"*** (Bahá'u'lláh, *Summons*, 97)

I'm sure you are reminded of Jesus' saying: ***"Foxes have holes and birds of the air have nests, but the Son of Man has no place to lay his head."*** (Mt 8:20) Apparently, such is the life that is led by most of the Manifestations of God.

QUESTION: Several times in your last book and in this one, you show a similarity between Jesus and Bahá'u'lláh, as to what they said. Does this mean that Bahá'u'lláh wasn't being original, or was even copying what Jesus said?

RESPONSE: Not at all. If we accept what the Bahá'í Faith is teaching about divine revelation, the words of the Manifestations are not their own words, but the Word of God. What they say is always original, but they may even quote scripture from a previous religion. Strikingly, (according to Christian scholars), Jesus is quoting or referring to the so-called Old Testament 15 to 20 per cent of the time when He speaks. But, nobody would accuse Jesus of being unoriginal.

The best example of the many times Jesus quotes Judaic scripture is the 'Great Commandment': ***"Teacher, which is the greatest commandment in the Law?" Jesus replied: "'Love the Lord your God with all your heart and with all your soul and with all your mind. This is the first and greatest commandment."*** (See Deut. 6:5 for the similar statement). Jesus said that there was a second commandment: ***'Love your neighbor as yourself. All the Law and the Prophets hang on these two commandments."*** (Mt 22: 36-40) Note that Jesus here refers to 'the Law and the Prophets' of the Jewish religion.

In passing, we can remember that the holy Qur'án references both Jesus and Mary frequently, as well as figures from the Old Testament, such as Moses and Joseph. So, it seems there is no issue with the Manifestations quoting or referring to previous Manifestations, since in the Bahá'í view there is only one God Who is speaking through all of them.

Bahá'u'lláh continues to tell the Shah: *"O King! I was but a man like others, asleep upon My couch, when lo, the breezes of the All-Glorious were wafted over Me, and taught Me the knowledge of all that hath been. This thing is not from Me, but from One Who is Almighty and All-Knowing. And He bade Me lift up My voice between earth and heaven, and for this there befell Me what hath caused the tears of every man of understanding to flow…This is but a leaf which the winds of the will of thy Lord, the Almighty, the All-Praised, have stirred. Can it be still when the tempestuous winds are blowing?…His all-compelling summons hath reached Me, and caused Me to speak His praise amidst all people…The hand of the will of thy Lord, the Compassionate, the Merciful, transformed Me."* (ibid. 97)

Bahá'u'lláh reveals a prayer for the Shah in which He asks God to *"remove the veils that have come in between Thee and Thy creatures and debarred them from turning unto the horizon of Thy Revelation."* He asks God to cause all men and women of the earth to *"turn from the left hand of oblivion and delusion unto the right hand of knowledge and certitude."* He begs God: *"O My God! Thou art the All-Bountiful, Whose grace is infinite.*

Withhold not Thy servants from the most mighty Ocean, which Thou hast made the repository of the pearls of Thy knowledge and Thy wisdom, and turn them not away from Thy gate, which Thou hast opened wide before all who are in Thy heaven and all who are on Thy earth.

"O Lord! Leave them not to themselves, for they understand not and flee from that which is better for them than all that Thou hast created upon Thine earth. Cast upon them, O My God, the glances of the eye of Thy favour and bounty, and deliver them from self and passion, that they may draw nigh unto Thy most exalted Horizon, taste the sweetness of Thy remembrance, and delight in that bread which Thou hast sent down from the heaven of Thy Will and the firmament of Thy grace. From everlasting Thy bounty hath embraced the entire creation and Thy mercy hath surpassed all things. No God is there but Thee, the Ever-Forgiving, the Most Compassionate. (Bahá'u'lláh, *Summons*, 2002, 103; all the above quotes are from *Summons*, 96-137)

Bahá'u'lláh prays for all human beings and the Shah in particular in this letter asking God to *"draw thereby the hearts of Thy creatures towards the heaven of Thy knowledge, and the heart of the Sovereign towards the right hand of the throne of Thy name, the All-Merciful. Supply him then, O My God, with a portion of that goodly sustenance which hath descended from the heaven of Thy generosity and the clouds of Thy mercy, that he may forsake his all and turn unto the court of Thy favour. Aid him, O My God, to assist Thy Cause and to exalt Thy Word amidst Thy creatures."* (ibid. 121)

QUESTION: Why does Bahá'u'lláh think He can ask a 'king' like the Shah to give up everything? This sounds presumptuous and grandiose.

RESPONSE: Well, I guess we have to remember that when the a person known in Christian history as the 'Rich Young Ruler' approached Christ, kneeling before Him and asking Him what he should do to inherit eternal life, Jesus tells him to obey the commandments. When the man says he has done this since he was a boy, Jesus adds: *"You still lack one thing. Sell everything you have and give to the poor, and you will have treasure in heaven. Then come, follow me."* (Lu 18:23)

I suspect neither you nor I would like to call Jesus presumptuous or grandiose. All the Manifestations seemingly knew what was in the hearts of those who approached them and Jesus evidently knew that shedding his fortune and following Christ in near poverty was what the 'Rich Young Ruler' needed spiritually. And Bahá'u'lláh must have known that the path to salvation for the Shah was to 'forsake his all.' And, by the way, Bahá'u'lláh also asked the Pope (see below) to do the same.

Bahá'u'lláh speaks of His continued imprisonment in this letter, then asks God to be a ransom for the spiritual 'self-imprisonment' of all the people of earth: *"We pray that, out of His bounty -- exalted be He -- He may release, through this imprisonment, the necks of men from chains and fetters, and cause them to turn, with sincere faces, towards His face, Who is the Mighty, the Bounteous."* (Bahá'u'lláh, Summons, 2002, 133)

In closing this letter to the Shah, Bahá'u'lláh speaks again of the tribulations He has borne and then utters a famous phrase that has been oft-quoted. He tells us: *"…I have been, most of the days of my life, even as a slave, sitting under a sword hanging on a thread, knowing not whether it would fall soon or late upon him."* (Bahá'u'lláh, Summons, 2002, 136) He prays to God: *"We further beseech God, exalted be He, to gather all mankind around the Gulf of the Most Great Ocean, an ocean every drop of which proclaimeth that He is the Harbinger of joy unto the world and the Quickener of all its peoples."* (ibid. 141)

Remembering that Jesus once referred to Himself as a 'temple,' Bahá'u'lláh closes by drawing an analogy from His life and teaching to the building of a temple, telling the Shah that this 'Temple' has been built through the power of His Revelation: **"Thus have We built the Temple with the hands of power and might, could ye but know it. This is the Temple promised unto you in the Book. Draw you nigh unto it. This is that which profiteth you, could ye but comprehend it. Be fair, O peoples of the earth! Which is preferable, this, or a temple which is built of clay? Set your faces towards it."** (ibid. 137) [51]

---

51 Once again, wikipedia.org has the best overall coverage of the Shah's life, with many pictures. Sadly, he will largely be remembered in the future, I believe, as the one who ordered the execution of the Báb and the imprisonment of Bahá'u'lláh in the 'Black Pit' of Teheran and His subsequent banishment to Baghdad.

POPE PIUS IX

Pope Pius IX

QUESTION: Bahá'u'lláh wrote, as you call them, a 'Tablet' to the Pope? Sounds fantastic, almost unbelievable.

RESPONSE: The word 'tablet' wasn't chosen by me. It has been in use since the 'Tablets of the Ten Commandments. 'Tablet' is just another word used in the middle-east, for an important letter, or in this case, a letter or message from a divine source (such as the 'tablets' of the Ten Commandments). Let me assure you that Bahá'u'lláh did write all these letters and copies of them exist in the Bahá'í International Archives. But back to the Tablet to Pope Pius IX, who served thirty-two years, longer than any other pope.

Baháʼuʼlláh said to him: *"O Pope! Rend the veils asunder. He who is the Lord of Lords is come overshadowed with clouds...He, Verily, hath come down from Heaven even as He came down from it the first time. Beware that thou dispute not with Him even as the Pharisees disputed with Him (Jesus) without a clear token or proof...seize thou the Cup of life with the hands of confidence, and first drink therefrom, and proffer it then to such as turn towards it amongst people of all faiths..."* (ibid. 54)

In one of the most striking passages, Baháʼuʼlláh reveals the following. Remember as you read this that Baháʼuʼlláh teaches that each Manifestation of God not only brings but actually *is* 'the Word of God.' This passage seems to refer to the time when Jesus gave Himself as a 'ransom' for the lives of men, followed by a passage where Baháʼuʼlláh reveals 'when We came once again,' indicating the reappearance and Return of Jesus, which Baháʼuʼlláh often states is seen in His own coming. Here is the passage:

"The Ancient of Days is come in His great glory! Hasten unto Him, O peoples of the earth, with humble and contrite hearts. Say: We, in truth, have given Ourself as a ransom for your own lives. Alas, when We came once again, We beheld you fleeing from Us, whereat the eye of My loving-kindness wept sore over My people. Fear God, O ye that perceive." (Baháʼuʼlláh, *Summons*, 2002, 57)

And: *"Rend asunder the veils of your idle fancies! This is your Lord, the Almighty, the All-Knowing, Who hath come to quicken the world and unite all who dwell on earth. Turn unto the Dayspring of Revelation, O people, and tarry not, be it for less than the twinkling of an eye. Read ye the Evangel* [the New Testament] *and yet refuse to acknowledge the All-Glorious Lord?"* (ibid. 58)

Bahá'u'lláh refers to Christ's statement to His disciples in John 16:12 that *"I have much more to say to you, more than you can now bear."* Bahá'u'lláh reveals: *"The Word which the Son concealed is made manifest. It hath been sent down in the form of the human temple in this day. Blessed be the Lord Who is the Father! He, verily, is come unto the nations in His most great majesty. Turn your faces towards Him, O concourse of the righteous!"* (ibid. 59)

One of the official titles of the Pope is 'the Successor of Peter, so it is not surprising that Bahá'u'lláh reveals the following, in which we hear Peter speaking: *"The Word which the Son concealed is made manifest…This is the day whereon the Rock (Peter) crieth out and shouteth, and celebrateth the praise of its Lord, the All-Possessing, the Most High, saying: 'Lo! The Father is come, and that which ye were promised in the Kingdom is fulfilled!'"* (Bahá'u'lláh, *The Proclamation of Bahá'u'lláh*, 1978, 84)

In the following paragraph, we see Bahá'u'lláh referring to Himself as the 'Pen' of God', a way of talking about Divine Revelation and showing that what is being said is not from Bahá'u'lláh, but from God. One of the titles of Bahá'u'lláh is the 'Most Great Name.' This portion of the message to Pope Pius IX states: *"Say: O peoples of all faiths! Walk not in the ways of them that followed the Pharisees and thus veiled themselves from the Spirit.* [i.e., Jesus] *They truly have strayed and are in error.*

The Ancient Beauty is come in His Most Great Name, and He wisheth to admit all mankind into His most holy Kingdom. The pure in heart behold the Kingdom of God manifest before His Face...Thus hath it been decreed by the Pen of the Ancient of Days, as bidden by Him Who is the Lord of the entire creation. He, verily, hath come again that ye might be redeemed, O peoples of the earth. Will ye slay Him Who desireth to grant you eternal life? Fear God, O ye who are endued with insight." (Bahá'u'lláh, *Summons*, 2002, 63)

And finally (though there is so very much more for Christian readers (whether Catholic or Protestant) in this Tablet that we referenced earlier. *"O Supreme Pontiff! Incline thine ear unto that which the Fashioner of mouldering bones conselleth thee...Sell all the embellished ornaments thou dost possess, and expend them in the path of God...Thus hath bidden thee He Who is the Possessor of Names, on the part of thy Lord, the Almighty, the All-Knowing."* (Bahá'u'lláh, *Proclamation, 1978, 84* [52]

QUESTION: Do the other 'Letters to the Kings' sound this same way?

RESPONSE: They do. All are very commanding to these Kings and don't forget the Queen, Victoria. Bahá'u'lláh was especially complimentary to her, as noted above.

---

52 Use britannica.com, the online Encyclopedia Britannica for a complete and detailed article on this Papacy. The 'Prisoner of the Vatican,' (so-called) will be remembered in Bahá'í history as one who ignored
the 'Summons' of Bahá'u'lláh. In current history books, he is remembered, among other things, for the doctrine of 'Infallibility' of the Papacy and for his construction of the 'Syllabus of Errors.'

CHAPTER 8

A Jazz Musician and a Famous African-American Scholar, both of whom became Bahá'ís. And a Botanist, Revered Arabic Scholar, a Russian Novelist, Middle-Eastern Scholar, and Two Presidents of Czechoslovakia. And, let's throw in an a Presidential Candidate and an Inventor

§

Jazz Musician John Birks 'Dizzy' Gillespie

'Dizzy' Gillespie (1913-1993) was not just a jazz musician, but a musical innovator, credited, along with others, of founding and promoting the 'bebop' style of music and Afro-Cuban jazz. With a scholarship, he studied harmony and theory at Laurinsburg Institute, in North Carolina early in his life and, the story goes, sneaked away from his Methodist Church on Sunday to attend the uninhibited 'Sanctified Church,' where he said: "I first learned the significance of rhythm there and all about how music can transport people spiritually." (Carr, I., Fairweather, D, Brian P, *The rough guide to Jazz*, 291)

Along with Charlie Parker, Bud Powell, Kenny Clarke, Thelonious Monk and Miles Davis, the 'bebop' style of composition and playing was invented. Later, Dizzy was centrally instrumental in the development of the Cuban Jazz idiom. Classics of Dizzy in bebop style were

A Night in Tunisia; Groovin' High; Salt Peanuts and *Dizzy's Dance*. In later life, he wrote an autobiography entitled: *To Be or Not…to Bop*.

Though he had already been aware of the Faith, he became a Bahá'í in 1968, after the deep personal shock he felt at Martin Luther King, Jr's assassination. From his autobiography, he tells us: "I believe that there is one God and He manifests Himself to mankind through great teachers for specific periods of time in our spiritual development, that He sends them periodically. It's like a relay runner who has a baton in his hand. You could look at the Word of God like a baton, the Holy Spirit. The runner grabs the baton and he runs and runs and runs; and while he runs that is the revelation of what's happening. When he gets to the end, he passes it on to the next guy, and he starts running with it, and that's the next religion. It's the same religion; it's just that a different prophet's running with it. He passes it to the next and the next and so on until there is peace and unity of mankind on earth as it is in Heaven.

"Becoming a Bahá'í changed my life in every way and gave me a new concept of the relationship between God and man – between man and his fellow man – man and his family. It's just all consuming. I became more spiritually aware, and when you're spiritually aware, that will be reflected in what you do. They teach you in the Bahá'í faith, without the idea of stopping you from doing things, to fill your life with doing something that's for real, and those other things you do, that are not for real, will fall off by themselves. I never needed to say, 'I'm gonna stop doing this.' I just found out that there was no time for it anymore. I started praying and reading a lot too. The (Bahá'í) writings gave me new insight on what the plan is – God's plan – for this time, the truth of the oneness of God, the truth of the oneness of the prophets, the truth of the oneness of mankind. That's it; that's what I learned." From his autobiography *To Be or Not…to Bop* (Gillespie, 1979, 474).

After becoming a Bahá'í, he gave up alcohol (he had never used drugs) and when challenged, he said: "It's a Bahá'í law and it's good for me." One commentator who knew him for forty years said Dizzy replaced alcohol with 'soul force.' He became a 'Jazz Ambassador' for the State Department, traveling to the middle-east and was often referred to as the 'Bahá'í Jazz Ambassador.' He visited Bahá'í homes and attended Bahá'í meetings wherever he went.

His favorite quote from Bahá'u'lláh was: "This earth is one country and mankind its citizens." He was at the Centenary of Bahá'u'lláh's announcement to the world of his mission held in 1963 in London and played a special jazz festival there, though he was not yet a declared Bahá'í. He had planned to be at the Centenary of Bahá'u'lláh's Ascension in New York in 1992, again to play a Jazz Festival as part of the celebration. However, he was by that time in the hospital, sick with pancreatic cancer. Frequently at the Bahá'í Center in New York, there is a 'jazz session' in his honor.[53]

BOTANIST AND HORTICULTURALIST, LUTHER BURBANK

He was the thirteenth of fifteen children, with a hardscrabble beginning and only an elementary education. Despite being denied the titles of 'scientist' and 'researcher' by the educational elite, Luther Burbank unfolded a life of discovery and practical contribution to

---

53 The legacy of Dizzy Gillespie is well displayed in wikipedia.org, including his Bahá'í affiliation. Additionally, there are several good interviews on You Tube, where Dizzy discusses his Bahá'í Faith.

the human race. His methods of grafting, hybridization and cross-breeding were groundbreaking and served to greatly increase the productive output for many kinds of produce. There are, to his credit, literally hundreds of varieties of fruits, grains, potatoes, tomatoes, ornamental flowers and other plants that appeared as 'new' and better, more productive types of foods and flowers. The list would be too long, but two of his greatest and most popular creations were the Shasta Daisy and the Russet Burbank potato. Even if you have not seen the beautiful Shasta Daisy (you probably have) you have eaten lots of Russet Potatoes!

Not well known, however, is Burbank's 'spiritual side.' His friend and admirer Paramahansa Yogananda said: "His heart was fathomlessly deep, long acquainted with humility, patience, sacrifice. His little home amid the roses was austerely simple; he knew the worthlessness of luxury, the joy of few possessions. The modesty with which he wore his scientific fame repeatedly reminded me of the trees that bend low with the burden of ripening fruits; it is the barren tree that lifts its head high in an empty boast." (From: bahaItributes.wordpress.com/luther-burbank)

Shortly before his death (1926), he gave a speech at the First Congregational Church of San Francisco, in which he said: "I love humanity, which has been a constant delight to me during all my seventy-seven years of life; and I love flowers, trees, animals, and all the works of Nature as they pass before us in time and space. What a joy life is when you have made a close working partnership with Nature, helping her to produce for the benefit of mankind new forms, colors, and perfumes in flowers which were never known before; fruits in form, size, and flavor never before seen on this globe; and grains of enormously increased productiveness, whose fat kernels are filled with more and better nourishment, a veritable storehouse of perfect food—new food for all the world's untold millions for all time to come." [54]

Burbank knew of the Bahá'í Faith, as did many leaders of thought around the turn of the century (see the section below describing the visit of a Secretary of State of the United States to 'Abdu'l-Bahá) and he left this tribute to the Faith of Bahá'u'lláh: "I am heartily in accord with the Bahá'í Movement, in which I have been interested for several years. The religion of peace is the religion that we need and always have needed, and in this Bahá'í is more truly the religion of peace than any other." (bahaitributes.wordpress.com)

QUESTION: Are you saying Burbank was a Bahá'í?

RESPONSE: His statement speaks for itself. Though he was not an official member of the Bahá'í Faith, his statement was made at a time when many people thought of themselves as Bahá'ís, even though they retained membership in a church (and even if they did not attend). It was only in the late twenties and early nineteen-thirties that Bahá'ís all over the world realized that an entirely new religion had begun to establish itself all over the world. Prior to the mid-1920's, many followers of Bahá'u'lláh who were Moslems attended the Mosque on Friday, as did 'Abdu'l-Bahá. Many North American Bahá'ís who were Christian not only attended Church on Sunday but were members of Churches. What changed this?

---

54 wikipedia,org/burbank

Ironically, it was a decision from an Egyptian court in the mid nineteen-twenties that held that the Bahá'ís of Egypt were not Muslims and could not be buried in Moslem cemeteries. That decision led the way to the realization of many Bahá'ís and those from outside the Bahá'í Faith that what now existed was not simply a movement, or a sect of another faith, but a completely new religion. Prior to this court decision, many people around the world thought of the Bahá'í Faith as a Muslim sect, probably in about the same way that a second or third century Roman thought of the Christian Faith as a 'Jewish sect.' Of course, Bahá'u'lláh and 'Abdul-Bahá had taught all along that this was a new Revelation from God and, thus, a new religion, not a sect of an already existing religion. But see below.

In a way, this was strikingly similar to what the followers of Jesus experienced in the several decades after Jesus' life had ended. They continued to worship in the synagogue as well as having their own special worship experiences recalling the life and teachings of Jesus. The book of Acts in the New Testament is very clear on the subject that many of Jesus' followers wanted to keep to the old Jewish ways of thought and worship, as well as acknowledgement of Jewish Law, and to combine this with their discipleship in Christ as an important addition to their age-old Jewish belief system.

After a time, however, two things happened. The Jews who were followers of Christ started to realize their uniqueness (just as the Bahá'ís did) and the Jewish religious hierarchy, fearful of their dynamism, excluded them (just as the Egyptian Islamic court did to the Bahá'ís).

So, at the close of the nineteenth century, and on up until the third decade of the twentieth century, there were a great many people who thought of themselves as both Christian and Bahá'í and may have attended Church and also attended Bahá'í 'Feasts' (which is what the periodic Bahá'í meetings are called).[55] Luther Burbank's statement makes him sound as if he may have been in this category. However, certainly by the mid 1930's, (or slightly earlier) the Bahá'ís realized that they were members of a new and different religion and thus no longer retained church memberships.

Bahá'ís who come from a Christian background often feel that it would have been a special gift to have been reared from birth in a Bahá'í home. On the other hand they often feel they have what could be called the 'best of both worlds.' They were disciples of Christ (many of whom had had a 'salvation in Christ' experience) and now they are followers of Bahá'u'lláh - Christ Returned. I have often thought of myself as having a 'dual-discipleship' with both Christ *and* Bahá'u'lláh. (Though followers of Baha'u'llah are not always called 'disciples.') And, my inclusive Bahá'í Faith also prompted me to revere and worship the 'Word of God' in the many other Manifestations of God Who have appeared in human history, including those such as Moses, Buddha, Muhammad, Zoroaster, and others.[56]

---

55 Bahá'ís gather every nineteen days for devotion, worship and consultative sharing within their community. The reason for nineteen days is that the Bahá'í Faith sets forth a new calendar of nineteen months, each containing nineteen days. Baha'is meet on the first of each of these months. FUN FACT: Early Christian meetings were also called 'Feasts.' Some denominations still call them that.

56 See encyclopedia.com/topic/Luther_Burbank for short description of Burbank's life and work.

An English Doctor Working in Jerusalem

Dr. Thomas Chaplin, in his late twenties, was working in Jerusalem, but while traveling to 'Akká in 1870, he met the Bahá'ís. While not meeting Bahá'u'lláh, he did have an opportunity to meet 'Abdu'l-Bahá, the son of Bahá'u'lláh. When asked by 'Abdu'l-Bahá why the Jews didn't recognize Christ when He came, Dr. Chaplin said he reckoned that they had misunderstood the scriptures. 'Abdu'l-Bahá replied to that by asking "…whether it might not be that Christians in like manner now misunderstood the scripture…" and thus were missing the appearance of Bahá'u'lláh, the Father of all mankind.

Dr. Chaplin added that "From all that I could learn, these people lead pure and harmless lives, and hold no political opinions which could render them dangerous," thus giving the lie to the story that had been told to the people of 'Akká that the new arrivals were dangerous political criminals. [57]

Well Known Christian Scholar in 'Akká

When Bahá'u'lláh arrived at 'Akká (Southern Syria at the time, now Northern Israel) the prison city was a place so foul that one story circulated that the air was so bad that if a bird flew over the city, it would drop from the sky. The prison-city was so unwholesome and filthy that people who were sent there were not expected to survive. Inside the walled city was what we would call a maximum-security prison. It was to this prison that Bahá'u'lláh was consigned. Only years later, was He allowed to live outside the prison, but inside the walled city proper, still under 'house arrest.'

---

57 Moojan Momen. *Bahá'u'lláh*, a Short Biography. (Oxford : Oneworld, 2007), 108.

Among the problems that anyone living in 'Akká faced was that there was no supply of drinkable water. The nearest well was ten minutes outside the city, but it gave only water with a bad taste. To find potable water, individuals had to travel over thirty minutes outside the city to a spring. Bahá'u'lláh showed concern over this situation immediately, not only for his family and followers (about seventy persons) but for all the people of the city.

Several years later, under house arrest, he suggested to the owner of the house in which he was living to consider building an aqueduct from a far-away spring to bring drinkable water to all in the city. The man's name was Ilyas Abbud, who was a wealthy Christian merchant. As such, he is a 'famous Christian' who played a part in Bahá'í history. Abbud lived next door to the portion of the house offered to Bahá'u'lláh.

At one point, Abbud was so wary and suspicious of the Persian exiles (who had been falsely portrayed as dangerous criminals) that he reinforced the wall between the portion of the house that he lived in from the section which housed Bahá'u'lláh. However, sometime later, as often happened, Abbud's view of Bahá'u'lláh was softened and he showed kindness and respect toward Him.

People who were around Bahá'u'lláh for any length of time, saw His character and His personality as outstanding and worthy of admiration and esteem. (Remember those weeping Christians we saw at the beginning of this book, who feared for Bahá'u'lláh's life at the time of his banishment from Edirne.) So, Abbud had asked if he could do any favor for Bahá'u'lláh, which is how Bahá'u'lláh's suggestion for an aqueduct came about.

But, back to the water problem: Abbud, though he could have afforded it, did nothing about the aqueduct. Later, Bahá'u'lláh was approached by the Governor of 'Akká, who had become an admirer. This Governor asked Bahá'u'lláh if he could do any favor for Him and Bahá'u'lláh replied that the city needed the aqueduct that He had earlier asked Abbud to build. The Governor responded and began almost immediately to build it. The aqueduct was finished only later when another Governor completed it. You can see portions of this aqueduct when you visit the Bahá'í Holy Places in Israel.

The point is, all the people of 'Akká were benefited by this aqueduct and none of them forgot how it came to be. They were thankful to Bahá'u'lláh, the prisoner, for all that He had done for them. From a beginning where they were angry and suspicious and wanted nothing to do with Bahá'u'lláh and His followers, they now held Him in the highest regard, revering Him and showing their love and gratitude. They realized that their city had changed in the few years that He had been in their midst.

So, finally, we come to the Christian scholar, whose name is (a name like Jacob) Ya'qub-ibn-Betros, from Lebanon. He was a renowned writer and a doctor of divinity and linguistics. When he was staying in 'Akká in the 1890's, (this was after Bahá'u'lláh ascended) he noticed the great change and transformation that had occurred there, especially the presence of fresh water. He wrote the following poetic composition and presented it to 'Abdu'l-Bahá, Bahá'u'lláh's son as a gift.

> 'Set betwixt the twin mounts of Lebanon and Carmel is the Bahji, [the Mansion of Bahji]

> Therein is the resting place of Baha, the Lord of Bounty and Mercy,
> The Chosen Master, the Lamp of Guidance, Baha -- the Splendour and the Light of the Sun of Truth,
> He Who is the Luminary of all names,
> Therein the true joy, the Desire of all hearts, hearts that seek His lights,
> The Solace of the eyes, the Fulfillment and Realization of all hope,
> By His beneficent presence, the water that springs from the wells of those parts was purified (i.e. of 'Akká) and the air and clime of 'Akká and its environs were changed.'

(Taherzedeh, *Revelation of Bahá'u'lláh*, vol. 3, 1983, 22)

In that last sentence of this Christian scholar's reverent remarks about the influence of Bahá'u'lláh, we see what was a common feeling among the inhabitants of 'Akká, namely, that because of Bahá'u'lláh's presence and His influence, the water, the air, even the climate of 'Akká had been changed.

INFLUENTIAL AFRICAN-AMERICAN SCHOLAR

Alain LeRoy Locke was an African-American writer, a scholar and patron of the arts, as well as an educator and philosopher.

QUESTION: Hold on, are you going to tell me that the famed Dr. Alain Locke became a Bahá'í? Are you making some of this up (sorry, just wondering)?

RESPONSE: He *did* become a Bahá'í. But here's my promise. None of what I share with you in this book is made up and everything I tell you about 'famous Christians' in the Bahá'í story is well researched and can be easily verified. Use the footnotes and look in the bibliography for other sources I have used. Dr. Locke was among the most famous scholars of the twentieth century of any race, and he was listed in a book *The Black 100* (Salley, 1993) as the 36th most influential Black person living in the twentieth century. He received far too many awards to mention, but let us recall that he was the first African-American Rhodes Scholar.

Alain Locke became a Bahá'í in 1918, the year he graduated from Harvard. He wrote to "Abdu'l-Baha and received a tablet from him. 'Abdu'l-Bahá had earlier asked a visiting pilgrim, Agnes Parsons, to host a Race Amity conference in Washington, DC. She did so, and Locke was a key participant.

In 1923, he made a pilgrimage to the Bahá'í World Center in Haifa. There, he met and later maintained contact with Shoghi Effendi, the twentieth century Guardian[58] and Head of the Bahá'í Faith. Shoghi Effendi even asked him to review his translation of Bahá'u'lláh's key text, *The Book of Certitude*. He also asked Locke to contribute to the Bahá'í World (a biennial publication). He wrote an essay entitled "The Orientation of Hope." In that essay, Locke states that the Bahá'í Faith is "a virile and truly prophetic spiritual revelation." [59]

Dr. Locke's years of appearance among us are 1885 - 1954. He is known for many things, especially his philosophical writings and for

---

[58] Shoghi Effendi Rabbani was appointed by 'Abdu'l-Bahá in his will as the sole leader, or 'Guardian' and Head of the Bahá'í Faith (from 1922 to 1957). The Universal House of Justice was elected in 1963.

[59] See planetbahai.org for an article by James Goldsmith dated 02/28/2003 from which this quote is taken.

his writing about the 'Harlem Renaissance.' He is credited by many as a motivating force for encouraging that movement and has even been referred to as the 'Father' or 'Dean' of the Harlem Renaissance. Several of those who participated in that renaissance spoke of his 'passion and energy' that seemed to infuse them with purpose and direction. Among many philosophical contributions from Dr. Locke, we should remember that he was the person who helped us begin to think about 'cultural pluralism,' the term he chose to highlight the need for cross-cultural knowledge and greater tolerance between cultural groups.

Dr. Alain LeRoy Locke

Dr. Locke wrote many moving passages on his chosen Bahá'í Faith. He said that what was needed today was "a revolution within the soul." He then spoke of Bahá'u'lláh's "trumpet call to humanity." From his perspective as a Bahá'í, he reminded us: "The word of God is still insistent, and more emphatic as human redemption delays and becomes more crucial..." (Quoted in planetbahai.org, Nov 19, 2009 issue) [60]

Middle-Eastern Scholar

Dr. E. G. Browne was among the most famous nineteenth century scholars of middle-eastern religions. He specialized in Persia [Iran], learned many languages, including Arabic and Farsi [the language of Iran], and both traveled and lived in Iran for an extended period. When he finally was granted an audience with Bahá'u'lláh, he seemed almost stunned. He said: "The face of him on whom I gazed I can never forget, though I cannot describe it. Those piercing eyes seemed to read one's very soul; power and authority sat on that ample brow...No need to ask in whose presence I stood, as I bowed myself before one who is the object of a devotion and love which kings might envy and emperors sigh for in vain!"

Though these are not Bahá'u'lláh's exact words, Dr. Browne tells us from his memory that Bahá'u'lláh said: "We desire but the good of the world and the happiness of the nations; yet they deem Us a stirrer up of strife and sedition worthy of bondage and banishment.... That all nations should become one in faith and all men as brothers; that the bonds of affection and unity between the sons of men should be strengthened; that diversity of religion should cease, and differences of race be annulled -- what harm is there in this?... Yet so it shall be; these fruitless strifes, these ruinous wars shall pass away,

---

60 See *Alain Locke: Race Leader, Social Philosopher, Bahá'í Pluralist*, in *World Order* 36:3 (2005), 7-36. Also see Alain Locke. *The New Negro*, An Interpretation. (New York: Albert and Charles Boni, 1925), for a book that signaled a 'turning point' for Black identity. Additionally, see Christopher Buck, *Alain Locke: Faith and Philosophy*, Kalimat Press, 2005.

and the 'Most Great Peace' shall come.... Yet do We see your kings and rulers lavishing their treasures more freely on means for the destruction of the human race than on that which would conduce to the happiness of mankind.... These strifes and this bloodshed and discord must cease, and all men be as one kindred and one family.... Let not a man glory in this, that he loves his country; let him rather glory in this, that he loves his kind...." (Bahá'u'lláh, *The Proclamation of Bahá'u'lláh*, 1978, viii)[61]

AN INTERNATIONALLY-KNOWN AUTHOR

Probably everyone has heard of Leo Tolstoy, the author of *War and Peace*, *Anna Karenina* and many other novels and philosophical writings. Let us quote him: (When you read this quote from Tolstoy, keep in mind that the Bahá'í Faith was known into the late 1800's by many as Bábism, meaning followers of the Báb, Bahá'u'lláhs predecessor) This is what he said: "The teachings of the Bábis. . . have a great future before them. "I therefore sympathize with Bábism with all my heart inasmuch as it teaches people brotherhood and equality and sacrifice of material life for service to God." And, he refers to Bahá'u'lláh's teachings in this way: "Bahá'u'lláh's teachings…now present us with the highest and purest form of religious teaching." (p. 35-6 of a pamphlet: *Appreciations of the Bahá'í Faith*, Bahá'í Publishing Committee, Wilmette, Illinois, 1941; also accessible on the web).

Tolstoy was in touch with Bahá'u'lláh's son, 'Abdu'l-Bahá, with the help of a Jewish merchant, Aziz Djazzab, who brought messages

---

61 Recommend Momen's article at: bahai-library.com/momen_encyclopedia_browne. Also, see Bahá'í scholar Hasan Balyuzi. *Edward Granville Browne and the Bahá'í Faith*.(Oxford: Oneworld, 1980) Additionally, see iranicaonline.org for more information.

back and forth. (Hmm? I have begun to run into more than a few Jews who played their part in the Bahá'í story. Is this another book emerging: Famous Jews: In Bahá'í history? One can wonder.)[62]

A Tap Dancer, And Other Artists And Entertainers

Maybe we should 'lighten up' from the scholars and internationally known authors and the like and deal with another entertainer. We already heard above about 'Dizzy' Gillespie, who became a Bahá'í, but there is another 'show biz' personality who could be mentioned as a famous Christian who decided to follow Bahá'u'lláh.

Fayard Nicholas

Fayard Nicholas was one half of the show business team known as the Nicholas Brothers, who created modern 'tap' as an entertainment

---

62 For information on Leo Tolstoy, wikipedia.org is excellent, with many pictures and references.

medium and dominated the field for many decades running from the 1920's through mid-century and beyond. Fayard was an inspiration to dancers Fred Astaire, Betty Grable, Donald O'Connor, Eleanor Powell and Ann Miller. He taught tap to all of them and influenced Michael Jackson! Donald O'Connor did a tap routine in the movie 'Singin' in the Rain' that was a homage to Fayard and was basically a copy of a part of Fayard's vaudeville act.

At age three, he was in the front row at vaudeville while his parents were playing in the orchestra. Teaching himself dance, then teaching his brother, by early teen years, he and his brother Harold were an act. An amazing career included being appreciated by the famed ballet master Balanchine, who invited him to be in a musical. In 2003, the Nicholas Brothers were named to the National Museum of Dance and Hall of Fame. They performed for nine presidents of the United States and numerous heads of state around the world. [63]

SOME OTHERS: There just isn't enough room in this book for all the artists and entertainers I would like to include, so here is a short list of some others who have adopted the Faith of Bahá'u'lláh: Actor Carole Lombard; Actor Alex Rocco; TV Actor Rainn Wilson of 'The Office'; Jim Seals and Dash Crofts of 'Seals and Crofts'; singer Vic Damone; Russell Garcia, film composer; Charles Wolcott, former MGM and Disney Studios Music Director, who won three Academy Awards; famed artist Mark Tobey. This list could be much longer, but this may give you a taste of those from the world of art and

---

[63] The Nicholas brothers have their own website: nicholasbrothers.com. Also, check out IMDB.com.

entertainment that have become followers of Bahá'u'lláh and have enlisted under the banner of the Bahá'í Revelation.

Two Presidents of Czechoslovakia

Czechoslovakia was, of course, in modern times split into the Czech Republic and the Slovak Republic, but when it was still just Czechoslovakia, its first President was former diplomat Tomas Masaryk, who said to the Bahá'ís: "Continue to do what you are doing, spread these principles of humanity and do not wait for the diplomats. Diplomats alone cannot bring the peace, but it is a great thing that official people begin to speak about these universal peace principles. Take these principles to the diplomats, to the universities and colleges and other schools, and also write about them. It is the people who will bring the universal peace." (From an audience with an American Bahá'í journalist in Praha, in 1928, quoted in Bahá'í Appreciations, reprinted from The Bahá'í World, Vol. VIII, Bahá'í Publishing Committee, Wilmette, Illinois, 1941)

Masaryk was succeeded by Edvard Benes, another diplomat and was the second president of Czechoslovakia (1935-1938). Forced out by the Nazis, he was for years, a President In Exile. His comment on the Bahá'í Faith was this: "I have followed it (the Bahá'í Cause) with deep interest ever since my trip to London to the First Races Congress in July, 1911, when I heard for the first time of the Bahá'í Movement and its summary of the principles for peace. I followed it during the war and after the war. The Bahá'í Teaching is one of the spiritual forces now absolutely necessary to put the spirit first in this battle against material forces.... The Bahá'í Teaching is one of the great instruments for the final victory of the spirit and of humanity.

"The Bahá'í Cause is one of the great moral and social forces in all the world today. I am more convinced than ever, with the increasing moral and political crises in the world, we must have greater international co-ordination. Such a movement as the Bahá'í Cause which paves the way for universal organization of peace is necessary." (From *Appreciations of the Bahá'í Faith*, as above.) [64]

William Jennings Bryan

Secretary of State And Presidental Candidate
Let me include William Jennings Bryan, Secretary of State under Woodrow Wilson and three time presidential candidate, known

---

64 For Masaryk, see britannica.com. For Benes, wikipedia.org is detailed and complete.

as 'The Great Commoner.' Though losing several runs for the presidency, he was a man of many accomplishments, and arguably one of the best speakers of the twentieth century. While a devout Christian, he was nevertheless among the many forward thinkers of the time who wanted to investigate the Bahá'í Cause. On a world tour in 1906, Bryan took time to make a visit to 'Abdu'l-Bahá, the son of Bahá'u'lláh, in Haifa, Palestine (now Israel). This shows that leaders of both thought and action were aware of what they called the Bahá'í 'movement,' not yet being aware that it was a new religion. Many were attracted because the Bahá'í teachings spoke so hopefully and practically about world peace and human unity.

When 'Abdu'l-Bahá was making his historic nearly one year tour of the United States in 1912, he stopped in Lincoln, Nebraska to visit Bryan's home, 'Fairview.' Bryan was not there, but 'Abdu'l-Bahá visited with his wife and daughter and wrote these words in the family guestbook: "Bless this family and grant it happiness in both this world and the world to come. Confirm this distinguished person in the greatest service to the human world, which is the unity of all mankind, that he may attain to Thy good pleasure in this world and obtain a bounteous portion from the surging ocean of Divine outpourings in this luminous age." [65]

AN INVENTOR: This person was much more than an inventor. His obituary described him as a lawyer, inventor, publisher, author

---

65 William Jennings Bryan was a fine man, with a long career of service to his country, that ended with a dramatic, if dubious, appearance as part of the prosecution at the Scopes 'Monkey' trial in 1925, opposite the legendary defense attorney, Clarence Darrow. wikipedia.org is comprehensive in its treatment of his life, including many good pictures.

and student of religion. His name is Arthur Pillsbury Dodge (1849-1915) I could add that he was an industrialist and an investor, but his main claim to fame was that he the first 'President' of the New York Bahá'í Community in 1898 and that he was a 'disciple' of 'Abdu'l-Bahá and was named by 'Abdu'l-Bahá as a 'Herald of the Kingdom.' All of this with no formal education, he was the example of that day of a 'self-made' man.

Arthur Dodge was a life-long seeker after truth. Shortly after the World's Fair in Chicago he was told, in 1895, about the 'Bahá'í teachings.' In a few years, before the turn of the century, he went on pilgrimage to 'Akká to visit 'Abdu'l-Bahá and came back fully confirmed to carry this message to the wider world.

Some of his exploits are so interesting. He was asked by Mary Baker Eddy to be her lawyer, but he declined. At another time, he teamed up with George Pullman to go into transportation. Sadly, at that time, street cars were being electrified and the steam approach which he and Pullman had favored did not materialize. Later, of course, when Dodge was no longer connected, Pullman became famous for railway cars.

Refusing to sell his inventions and investment approaches for an offer of over a million dollars, Dodge later lost nearly everything in a stock market crash. He managed to save his Manhattan home and when 'Abdu'l-Bahá visited the United States in 1912 Dodge hosted the Master in his home several times. He founded several magazines, including the well-respected *New England Magazine*, and published several books of his own, including: *The Truth of It: The Inseparable Oneness of Common Sense*, which was the first book on the

Bahá'í Faith written by a western Bahá'í. Another of his books was called: *Whence, Why, Whither? Man, Things, Other Things* in which he explored the 'nature, purpose and direction of human existence.'

Arthur Pillsbury Dodge said before he died that his only regret was "that he could not live long enough to complete his work for the Blessed Cause, to serve God and Man as he never had been able to do." It is hard to know what he meant by this, since his service was so outstanding. 'Abdul-Baha had the last word on Dodge, saying in a letter to his family:

"In reality that honorable soul served the Cause of God and endured many hardships and vicissitudes. His services are registered in the everlasting book in the Kingdom of God and mentioned by the Supreme Concourse. They shall never be forgotten. Ere long they will yield great results and will become the means of happiness to that household and conducive to the honor of its members. I will never forget him and supplicate for him graces and bounties from His Highness the Almighty…Although his star set in the horizon of this world yet he dawned with the utmost brilliancy from the horizon of eternity." The gravestone of Arthur Pillsbury Dodge shows the 'Greatest Name' Bahá'í symbol.[66]

---

[66] For more on Arthur P. Dodge, and for the source of quotations in this section, see bahai-library/?file=francis_dodge_biography. Also: *Star of the West* magazine, April 9, 1911, Vol. 19.

Finally, see: bahai-encyclopedia-project.org/index.php?=com_content& view=ar

CHAPTER 9

Some Nameless but nevertheless Famous Christians

§

QUESTION: WAIT A MINUTE. IF these people have no names, why include them among 'famous Christians'?

RESPONSE: Let me explain. There are persons in the Bible, in the New Testament, who are famous to us now, both for just being a person in the Bible, and also for what they did, or some part that they played, in this case, in the life of Jesus. Let me give you two examples.

THE WOMAN AT THE WELL

First, there is 'the woman at the well.' We don't know her name, but we do know that she encountered Jesus there when she came with a skin to draw water for her family. Here is the story, from the Gospel of John 4: 1-26.

"Now Jesus learned that the Pharisees had heard that he was gaining and baptizing more disciples than John—although in fact it was not Jesus who baptized, but his disciples. So he left Judea and went back once more to Galilee. Now he had to go through Samaria. So he came to a town in Samaria called Sychar, near the plot of ground Jacob had given to his son Joseph. Jacob's well was there, and Jesus, tired as he was from the journey, sat down by the well. It was about noon.

"When a Samaritan woman came to draw water, Jesus said to her, *'Will you give me a drink?'* (His disciples had gone into the town to buy food.) The Samaritan woman said to him, 'You are a Jew and I am a Samaritan woman. How can you ask me for a drink?' (For Jews do not associate with Samaritans.)

"Jesus answered her, *'If you knew the gift of God and who it is that asks you for a drink, you would have asked him and he would have given you living water.'* 'Sir,' the woman said, 'you have nothing to draw with and the well is deep. Where can you get this living water? Are you greater than our father Jacob, who gave us the well and drank from it himself, as did also his sons and his livestock?'

"Jesus answered, *"Everyone who drinks this water will be thirsty again, but whoever drinks the water I give them will never thirst. Indeed, the water I give them will become in them a spring of water welling up to eternal life.'* 'The woman said to him, 'Sir, give me this water so that I won't get thirsty and have to keep coming here to draw water…'

"The woman said, "I know that Messiah" (called Christ) "is coming. When he comes, he will explain everything to us." Then Jesus declared, *'I, the one speaking to you—I am he.'"*

Wouldn't you agree that this woman is famous, even though we don't know her name? Here's another example, a Canaanite woman. She's equally famous, but has no name.

The Canaanite Woman

From Mt 15: 1 – 28: "Leaving that place, Jesus withdrew to the region of Tyre and Sidon. A Canaanite woman from that vicinity came to him, crying out, 'Lord, Son of David, have mercy on me! My daughter is suffering terribly from demon-possession.' [Author's note: In ancient times, mental illness was thought to be possession by demons. This continued well into the twentieth century.]

"Jesus did not answer a word. So his disciples came to him and urged him, 'Send her away, for she keeps crying out after us.' He answered, *'I was sent to the lost sheep of Israel.'* 'Lord, help me!' she said. He replied, *'It is not right to take the children's bread and toss it to their dogs.'*

"'Yes, Lord,' she said, 'but even the dogs eat the crumbs that fall from their master's table.' Then Jesus answered, *'Woman you have great faith! Your request is granted.'* And her daughter was healed from that very hour."

Author's Note: If Jesus seems uncharacteristically harsh in his reply to this woman, we should remember that early in Jesus' ministry, he made several statements that his ministry was first and foremost (or even only) to the Jews. It was sometime later, when He apparently felt that his disciples could begin to understand that His message was universal, that Jesus told his disciples that His Faith was to be taken into 'all the world.'

And Jesus may have been testing the faith of the Canaanite woman. Apparently she passed the test! And, if you are wondering why the disciples wanted to send the woman away, the Jews of that time had laws about ritual purity that did not allow them to drink, eat or associate with those who were not Jewish. Jesus, of course, had no such compunction, either with this woman or the woman at the well, both non-Jews.

QUESTION: All right, I get it. You can be nameless, but still famous. Who are these nameless, famous Christians? I guess you are going to tell me they are famous because of their association with Bahá'u'lláh?

RESPONSE: Exactly, just as the woman at the well and the Canaanite woman are famous to Christians because of their encounters with Jesus.

A Christian Bishop

There was a Christian Bishop in Istanbul (Constantinople) who wrote a letter to Bahá'u'lláh, while Bahá'u'lláh was in Edirne, asking certain questions. We think he was an Orthodox Bishop, but we don't know his name.[67] And, sadly, we do not have a copy of that letter, but apparently he was asking Bahá'u'lláh of His view of Christ. The reply that the Bishop received contains one of the most famous passages in the Bahá'í Revelation and, as many people have remarked, one of the most moving and reverential statements ever made about Jesus, even including all of Christian literature. Here is that statement:

"Know thou that when the Son of Man yielded up His breath to God, the whole creation wept with a great weeping. By sacrificing

---

[67] See Adib Taherzadeh. *The Revelation of Bahá'u'lláh*. (Oxford, Ronald, 1988), vol. 4, 243.

Himself, however, a fresh capacity was infused into all created things. Its evidences, as witnessed in all the peoples of the earth, are now manifest before thee. The deepest wisdom which the sages have uttered, the profoundest learning which any mind hath unfolded, the arts which the ablest hands have produced, the influence exerted by the most potent of rulers, are but manifestations of the quickening power released by His transcendent, His all-pervasive, and resplendent Spirit.

"We testify that when He came into the world, He shed the splendor of His glory upon all created things. Through Him the leper recovered from the leprosy of perversity and ignorance. Through Him, the unchaste and wayward were healed. Through His power, born of Almighty God, the eyes of the blind were opened, and the soul of the sinner sanctified. Leprosy may be interpreted as any veil that interveneth between man and the recognition of the Lord, his God. Whoso alloweth himself to be shut out from Him is indeed a leper, who shall not be remembered in the Kingdom of God, the Mighty, the All-Praised. We bear witness that through the power of the Word of God every leper was cleansed, every sickness was healed, every human infirmity was banished. He it is Who purified the world. Blessed is the man who, with a face beaming with light, hath turned towards Him." Bahá'u'lláh, *Gleanings*, 1939, 85)

CHRISTIANS WHO SENT FOOD TO MARTYRS' FAMILIES

A few moments ago, we discussed the fact that Bahá'ís have been imprisoned and executed in Persia/Iran for their beliefs throughout their history. At times, these persecutions have been intense, as in the city of Yazd, Persia, in the late 1880's. Seven men were offered an opportunity to deny their Faith in Bahá'u'lláh. When they refused, and even continued to openly proclaim their Faith, they were executed in bizarre ways, including strangling, beheading and cutting of throats. The first to die was a young man in his early twenties, who was strangled. Another martyr was in his mid-eighties. Here is a description of the event:

"Amongst other instances, with chains and fetters, swords and scimitars, they dragged seven men, to whose purity, nobility, excellence, and virtue all bore witness, who had never in their lives injured even an ant, and against whom nothing could be alleged save that they were Bábís, before a few ignorant wretches like unto Annas and Caiaphas who account themselves learned, and commanded them to disavow their connection with this creed. When they refused to do this, and indeed confessed and admitted it, they beheaded each of these poor oppressed ones in a public thoroughfare, affixed them to gibbets, dragged their bodies with ropes through the streets and bázárs, and at length cut them in fragments and burned them with fire. Some others they spirited away, and it is not known what sufferings were inflicted upon them. About a thousand persons have fled from Yazd into the wilderness and open country, some have died from thirst in the mountains and plains, and all their possessions have been plundered and spoiled.

"Oppression and tyranny have so destroyed and uprooted these poor oppressed people that for several days the families and wives and children of the murdered men were weeping, sorrowing, and shivering, hungry and thirsty, in underground cellars, unable even to ask for water; none had any pity for them, but only blows; and indeed the common people, incited and goaded on by the clergy and the government, strove to injure them in every way, in which endeavour they showed neither ruth nor remission.

"Only after some days <u>certain Christian merchants who were passing through Yazd brought bread and water for the children of the victims...</u>" [Underlining by author]

(As seen in bahai-library.com: Persecutions of Bábis in 1888-1891 at Isfahan and Yazd. Originally published in *Materials for the Study of the Bábi and Bahá'í Religions*, E.G. Browne, 1918)

Because of Tolstoy's interest in the Bábi movement and because several middle-eastern scholars had written about these developments and, additionally, because the intelligentsia of western nations took interest, these actions in Yazd became widely known around the world. Bahá'u'lláh was so saddened by this incident that He revealed nothing for nine days and would see no one. Then He did something extraordinary: He wrote a Tablet (a letter) to the London Times, detailing the suffering of the Bahá'ís in Iran and calling upon the Times and all the newspapers of the world to be aware of this suffering and to call upon rulers to alleviate it. (Apparently, as far as is known, this is the first example in history of divine revelation initially appearing in a newspaper.) Here is a portion of that Tablet:

"O 'Times', O thou endowed with the power of utterance! O dawning place of news! Spend an hour with the oppressed of Iran, and witness how the exemplars of justice and equity are sorely tried beneath the sword of tyrants. Infants have been deprived of milk,

and women and children have fallen captive to the lawless. The blood of God's lovers hath dyed the earth red, and the sighs of His near ones have set the universe ablaze.

"O assemblage of rulers, ye are the manifestations of power and might, and the fountainheads of the glory, greatness and authority of God Himself. Gaze upon the plight of the wronged ones. O day-springs of justice, the fierce gales of rancour and hatred have extinguished the lamps of virtue and piety. At dawn, the gentle breeze of divine compassion hath wafted over charred and cast-out bodies, whispering these exalted words: 'Woe, woe unto you, O people of Iran! Ye have spilled the blood of your own friends and yet remain in ignorance of what ye have done. Should ye become aware of the deeds ye have perpetrated, ye would flee to the desert and bewail your crimes and tyranny.'

"O misguided ones, what sin have the little children committed? Hath anyone, in these days, had pity on the dependents of the oppressed? <u>A report hath reached Us that the followers of the Spirit (Christ) – may the peace of God and His mercy be upon Him -- secretly sent them provisions and befriended them out of utmost sympathy</u>. [Underlining from author] *We beseech God the Eternal Truth, to confirm all in accomplishing that which is pleasing to Him. O newspapers published throughout the cities and countries of the world! Have ye heard the groan of the downtrodden, and have their cries of anguish reached your ears? Or have these remained concealed? It is hoped that ye will investigate the truth of what hath occurred and vindicate it . . ."*

(Taherzadeh, *Revelation of Bahá'u'lláh*, vol. 4, 1987, 350)

My guess is that you are thinking what I am thinking, about the time Jesus spoke to His disciples about His Return, saying that at that time, He would say to them: ***"Come, you who are blessed by my Father; take your inheritance, the kingdom prepared for you since the creation of the world. For I was hungry and you gave me something to eat, I was thirsty and you gave me something to drink, I was a stranger and you invited me in, I needed clothes and you clothed me, I was sick and you looked after me, I was in prison and you came to visit me.***

"Then the righteous will answer him, 'Lord, when did we see you hungry and feed you, or thirsty and give you something to drink? When did we see you a stranger and invite you in, or needing clothes and clothe you? When did we see you sick or in prison and go to visit you?' "The King [i.e., Jesus] will reply, ***'I tell you the truth, whatever you did for one of the least of these brothers of mine, you did for me.'*** (Mt 25:35-46)

Jesus apparently was teaching that at the time of Judgement, there would be a separation of people between sheep and goats, with the goats being those who would not help others, the sheep being the empathetic helpers. Well, now it seems we can better understand those Christians who decided to help the Bahá'í families who had no food or water. They simply wanted to follow the teaching of Christ, to help those who were in need. Thank goodness for this Christian teaching, from which has flowed many charitable impulses and institutions.

Though we don't know their names, the Christians who helped the desperate Bahá'ís on this occasion are truly 'famous' to me, and I hope to you. I am assured that their names are known in Heaven and that 'the King' rewarded them.

CHRISTIANS WHO GAVE HOSPITALITY TO BAHÁ'ÍS

When Bahá'u'lláh was being further exiled from Baghdad to Constantinople, now Istanbul, He was hosted on separate occasions by several different Christian families. We do not know their names, nor do we know why or how this happened. There is a mystery, isn't there, as to why He was offered hospitality from Christians when those Christians were a distinct minority of the population, probably less than five percent of the total?

The record does not help us on this. We are left to speculate and I am immediately taken back to Bahá'u'lláh's comment or question as to why the Christians in Edirne (back in Chapter One) were weeping more loudly than others. Did He seek out these Christians? Did they seek Him out? We do not know. [68]

What we *do* know are three things: First, that Christians had developed traditions of hospitality and charity based on Jewish and Christian scripture and the teachings of Jesus. Therefore, maybe they were simply acting out their beliefs, being 'Christ-like,' so to speak. There is, as you are starting to see, a 'fabric' of connection between Christians and Bahá'u'lláh. This hosting of Bahá'u'lláh may be a thread in that fabric.

---

[68] They are only mentioned in passing in several Bahá'í histories, including Taherzadeh's *The Revelation of Bahá'u'lláh*.

Second, by now we see an obvious fact, that Bahá'u'lláh acknowledged Christians as capable of being emotionally responsive to Him and it seems that at least some Christians were at ease around Him. Did these Christians recognize 'something' familiar about Him, even if they did not recognize His specific claim to be the spiritual Return of their Savior? It is not until later (and later in this book) that we hear of the first Christian to declare Faith in Bahá'u'lláh, but perhaps these hospitable Christians were a precursor to those many Christians who would later find Christ in their midst in the Person of Bahá'u'lláh.

Third, and finally, it is clear that, just as with Jesus, Bahá'u'lláh's 'outreach' to humanity knew no boundaries or limits. He came, He suffered, He taught, was banished, imprisoned and tortured for all humanity, not just for certain groups or religions. Nonetheless, having said this, Bahá'u'lláh seems to have reached out to Christians in a 'special' and unique way. He certainly did write to Zoroastrians, Jews and Muslims, inviting them to recognize Him as the Manifestation for this Day. However, we are not aware that He wrote a personal letter of such direct appeal to any other religious group, compared to the letter He wrote to Christians. That letter, entitled the 'Most Holy Tablet,' but often referred to as 'Letter to the Christians,' stands out as atypical and extraordinary in its strong appeal to Christian believers. (It is included in a later chapter.)

Jesus expected and hoped that His people, the Jews, would be the first to accept His message, even saying early in His ministry that His Message was directed precisely toward the Jewish nation, not to others. Of course, He later asked His disciples to take the message into 'all the world.' Likewise, Bahá'u'lláh appealed to the people of

His own faith, the Muslims, to respond readily to His message, but this did not occur in mass numbers, just as the Jews did not respond to Jesus. In both cases, nearly all of the early adherents of Jesus were Jews, and Bahá'u'lláh's early followers were nearly all Muslims, with a few Zoroastrians and Jews also following Him. Nevertheless, within a century or two after Christ's Ascension, most Christians were Gentiles and in a century and a half, most of Bahá'u'lláh's disciples were non-Muslim.

Bahá'u'lláh certainly did say in an unequivocal and resounding manner that the Revelation of God that He brought in His Person was for all humanity. Even so, there is that seemingly special connection between Bahá'u'lláh and Christian believers, which, by the way, is the key reason why this book - *Famous Christians*- was written.

A Maid who Fainted

When Bahá'u'lláh was informed that He and his family and followers were to be exiled from Edirne (Adrianople), Turkey to 'Akká, in Syria (now Israel), one of his followers, a man named Haji Ja'far, was so deeply troubled in hearing that he would not be able to accompany Bahá'u'lláh, that he became seriously depressed. To understand Ja'far, you can compare how you think a disciple of Jesus – John the 'Beloved Disciple' perhaps – would have felt if he had been told that he would never see Jesus again.

Though Bahá'ís had been directed by Bahá'u'lláh not to attempt suicide under any circumstances, Ja'far was inconsolable and believing he would never see his Lord again, he did the unthinkable and cut his throat with a razor.

When he was being reassured that a surgeon would be there soon, he kept saying he did not want medical attention, but wanted to die because, as he put it, "...away from my Beloved, this life is useless to me." Though it was later determined that the carotid artery had not been severed, the scene was confused and shockingly bloody. One person who came to see what all the shouting was about immediately fainted. Then another person was sent from the kitchen to find out what was happening. This was a Christian maid, who also fainted on the spot. [69]

This story is told for two reasons. First, to show that there was contact of all kinds between Christians and Bahá'ís, from Archbishops to Monks to Bishops to 'maids.' Bahá'ís and Bahá'u'lláh had contact with friends, merchants, employees, landlords, and government officials who were Christian. The second reason is for us to be reminded that, just as it was for Christians during the early centuries, many thousands of Bahá'ís had relinquished their lives in martyrdom during persecutions that occurred in Persia during the second half of the nineteenth century. Almost unbelievably, this continues even today, with both imprisonments as late as 2009. In the last four decades, there have been persecutions, imprisonments and executions for no other reason than being followers of Bahá'u'lláh. There have been no executions in recent years, but Baha'is in Iran know that they are, as Baha'u'llah once described Himself, **"sitting under a sword hanging on a thread."** (Baha'u'llah, Epistle to the Son of the Wolf, p. 94)

---

[69] See Adib Taherzadeh. *The Revelation of Bahá'u'lláh* (Oxford, Ronald, 1977), vol. 2, 407.

While Ja'far was not a martyr, his story shows the readiness to relinquish life for his desire to be a faithful follower of Bahá'u'lláh, as well as the centrality that Bahá'u'lláh occupied in his life. Christians will understand this well, I know, since they feel something similar if not identical to that which Ja'far felt. For my own father and mother, and for me, Christ was always at the center of our lives and thought. That 'Center' was there from the earliest time of my life. Now, I feel privileged to have Christ still at the center, in the Person of Bahá'u'lláh, whom I believe to be Christ Returned.

As for Haji Ja'far, Bahá'u'lláh came to his bedside later, lovingly assuring him that he would be able to come to 'Akká as soon as his wounds were healed; he and his brother did, in fact, come to 'Akká within several months. (Taherzadeh, *The Revelation of Bahá'u'lláh*, vol. 2, 407)

A Christian Priest Weeps as two Bahá'í Brothers are Martyred

The background here is another story of martyrdom. In the city of Isfahan, Persia (Iran), there was a general persecution of Bahá'ís occurring and an evil-minded man took what he saw as an opportunity to reduce a large debt that he owed to two well-known and well-loved merchants who were followers of Bahá'u'lláh. He arranged for religious leaders and the general populace to arrest them and finally, to kill them.

The two brothers were named Hasan and Husayn, but they are known in Bahá'í history as 'the King of Martyrs' and 'the Beloved of Martyrs.' They were arrested, chained, then taken before religious authorities for pronouncement of a death sentence, then beheaded. (Remind you of anyone in the New Testament?) Their homes were plundered and all their possessions confiscated. Bahá'u'lláh spoke of them frequently in Tablets that He revealed, extolling their service to what He often called 'The Cause of God.'

'Abdu'l-Bahá wrote this: *"Indeed in such wise was the blood of these two brothers shed that even the Christian priest of Julfa* [a district of Isfahan] *cried out, lamented, and wept on that day; and this event befell after such sort that everyone wept over the fate of those two brothers, for during the whole period of their life they had never distressed the feelings even of an ant, while by general report they had in the time of the famine in Persia spent all their wealth in relieving the poor and distressed. Yet, notwithstanding this reputation, were they slain with such cruelty in the midst of the people!* (Abdu'l-Baha, *A Traveler's Narrative*, 1980, 92) [70]

Templers who Settled on MT Carmel

Before we get to the 'Templers,' who were German, let's discuss generally the fact that Christians all over the world expected the imminent Return of Christ in the mid 1840's. Rev. William Miller, among others, even chose what he thought would be the exact date and the sense of expectation of this event was strong, especially in Europe and even more so in the United States. Sermons were preached, speeches made in Congress, books written and some even sold their possessions and went to mountaintops, forming communities who were hopeful and watchful for this event, which was thought to be immediate. Though different opinions exist as to what Miller did and didn't do, he did specify that he thought Christ's return would be between April 21, 1843 and April 21 of 1844.

---

70 For more information, see Shoghi Effendi's history of the Bahá'í Faith's first century, *God Passes By*. (Wilmette, IL: Bahá'í Publishing Company, 1944), 200.

When the first date he picked in 1843 yielded no event, he consulted the Bible again and discovered, he said, that he had made a mathematical error and the year would be 1844 [71] (this was the year that the Bahá'í Faith began!). 1844 came and went without event, or so Miller and his disciples thought. Little did they know that the beginning of a new Faith was at hand which would, indeed, signal the Return of the Spirit of Christ, namely, Bahá'u'lláh.

The 'Millerites,' as they were then known, were greatly disappointed. However, several religious groups developed from the ferment and excitement of their movement, among them the Seventh-Day Adventists and the Jehovah's Witnesses. One wonders whether, someday, these groups will take another look at their history, to discover that Miller was (!) right, not wrong, and consider following Bahá'u'lláh, as Christ Returned in the Glory of the Father. I guess this makes Miller a 'famous Christian,' doesn't it, for getting the date right, and for realizing that Jesus' Return was imminent. He was *so close* to recognition of God's new Manifestation in the person of Bahá'u'lláh. [72]

In the letter which Bahá'u'lláh wrote to all Christians (and therefore to you), he asks: **"Tell Me then: Do the sons** [that is, the Christians] **recognize the Father, and acknowledge Him, or do they deny Him,**

---

[71] There is confusion on this point. After the specified date passed, Miller and others world-wide began hoping for a new date in October, 1844, but still no return, as far as they knew. Of course, the Báb had appeared, with Bahá'u'lláh as one of His followers, in May, 1844, near Miller's first date range. One of the best summaries about 'millennial Christians' can be found in Cedarquist, *The Story of Bahá'u'lláh*, 2005, appendix 4, p. 296f.

[72] Miller's life and work are well recorded on wikipedia.org, including references to various biographies.

***even as the people aforetime denied Him (Jesus)?*"** This letter is included later in this book. (Bahá'u'lláh, *Tablets of Bahá'u'lláh*, 1978, 14)

QUESTION: Are you going to get to the 'Templars'?

RESPONSE: Well, the words are very similar, so pardon me for correcting you. It's not the 'Templars' we are talking about. Templars (as opposed to 'Templers') were a military order that was among the most famous of the Christian fighters of the Crusades. They were organized in the twelfth century and were disbanded in less than one hundred years. Their common name was: Knights Templar, the Order of the Temple (of Solomon). Another designation was 'Fellow Soldiers of Christ.'

So, as you ask, let's talk about the 'Templers,' Germans who, because of their intense millennial views, were put out of their Lutheran tradition. They felt, as did Rev. Miller in the United States, that Christ's Return was imminent. (Interestingly, Christians in many parts of the world had come to this conclusion at about the same time.) The Templers were less certain about the date, but thought it would be in the 1870's or 1880's. However, about one thing they were certain: Christ, when he returned, would surely return to the Holy Land. And, they thought, where else would be the most likely place of His return than Mt. Carmel, the 'Mountain of the Lord,' in what is now northern Israel, which is the seat of the World Center of the Bahá'í Faith?

One leader of the Templers was Georg David Hardegg. He and others immigrated to Haifa, Israel (the city at the foot of Mr. Carmel, the 'Mountain of the Lord' in the Old Testament and the haunt of Elijah). Here are several ironies: Their one and only reason for going to the Holy Land was to be there when Christ returned. Hardegg actually wrote a letter to Bahá'u'lláh and received a reply. Also, Bahá'u'lláh, after his imprisonment in the prison city of 'Akká was 'relaxed,' was allowed to travel to nearby Haifa several times. On one of those occasions, He even stayed in one of the Templer's houses.[73]

And, the final irony:

Above one of the doorways of a Templer house, there was the inscription: "Der Herr is Nahe," meaning, "The Lord is Near." Amazingly, they were so right and so close, but they missed Him. Right about the time and place, but still oblivious to exactly Who it was that had been in their very midst. The Templer Colony is still there in Haifa, and that famous inscription can still be seen. Here's my speculation: In the next life, I guess Hardegg and his followers are able to be happy about being 'mostly right' (about the place and the time of Christ's Return) and happy now to be united with the Lord they sought so diligently. [74]

Two Christian Servants

When Bahá'u'lláh was further exiled from Baghdad to Constantinople, where he spent only four months, he was initially provided a house

---

73 See Adib Taherzadeh, *The Revelation of Bahá'u'lláh*. (Oxford, Ronald, 1988), vol. 4, p. 351.

74 wikipedia.org is very helpful in describing this movement. Sadly, many of the Templers devolved into Nazi supporters during the Second World War. Failure to recognize Bahá'u'lláh as the Return of Christ they so keenly sought, may have sapped them of the obvious vitality displayed in their early years.

for his family and followers. The government also provided two Christian servants, who could attend to shopping and other needs of the Bahá'í group. We know about them, because the record shows that a tent was pitched for them in the courtyard outside the house. [75]

We don't know the names of these two servants, but it is interesting to speculate about the interaction between them and the Bahá'ís. The New Testament 'woman at the well' or the Canaanite woman who sought healing for her daughter were physically close to Jesus; like them, these two servants must have been around Bahá'u'lláh at some point, must have seen or talked to Him. Were their lives changed? I wonder?

Missionary Inquiring about Muhammad

In the late 1800's, an unnamed missionary came to talk to the father of Adib Taherzadeh. Adib is the author of a masterful four volume historical work entitled *The Revelation of Bahá'u'lláh*. The missionary, who knew the Persian language well, was inquiring of Adib's father about the mission of Muhammad and about the authenticity of Bahá'u'lláh's mission and revelation. Missionaries to Iran were often quite interested in the Bahá'í Revelation; the reason may have been that they heard the 'accent' of Jesus' voice in the voice of Bahá'u'lláh and recognized the similarity of Christian teaching and Bahá'í beliefs and principles.

In the interview, the missionary is seen to be generally reasonable, but inclined to denigrate Muhammad. The irony of this is that

---

[75] See AdibTaherzadeh. *The Revelation of Bahá'u'lláh*. (Oxford, Ronald, 1977 vol. 2, p. 3.

missionaries in Iran made little headway, largely because they did not carefully read the Qur'án. In that Holy Book, Christ is frequently mentioned, defended and extolled and, interestingly, there is much more material about Mary, the Mother of Christ, as compared with the Bible. So, when missionaries told prospective converts that Muhammad was a 'false prophet,' this seemed confusing and contradictory to their listeners, who were aware of the Qur'án's promotion of Jesus as having brought a divine message from God. [76]

Two Christian Merchants in 'Akká

The first merchant does have a name. He is 'Udi Khammar, who owned various properties in 'Akká and also a mansion two miles north of 'Akká. Early in the 'Akká period, after Bahá'u'lláh was released from the prison, but was still under house arrest in the 'prison-city,' 'Udi Khammar supplied the house that Bahá'u'lláh lived in starting in 1871. Later still, after an epidemic of disease (probably bubonic plague) drove many people from the environs of 'Akká and the countryside surrounding it, 'Udi Khammar fled his mansion.

Bahá'u'lláh moved to this mansion, called Bahji, (the word means 'Delight') in 1879 and remained there for the rest of His earthly life. However, He once said to a companion that even though the mansion of Bahji was wonderful, he would prefer to be back in what He called 'The Most Great Prison' because He had become used to it. At other times, He told friends that he had become accustomed to the adversity and suffering that had been brought into His life by the Will of God.

---

76 ibid., 21

When 'Udi Khammar built this beautiful mansion, and years before Bahá'u'lláh occupied it, he had the following inscription placed over the entrance: "Greetings and salutations rest upon this mansion which increaseth in splendor through the passage of time. Manifold wonders and marvels are found therein, and pens are baffled in attempting to describe them." This inscription seems to foreshadow in an eerie way the arrival of Bahá'u'lláh and all that was to transpire while He was there. (Taherzadeh, *The Revelation of Bahá'u'lláh*, 1987, vol. 4, 104) [77]

ANOTHER MERCHANT

Our other Christian merchant does not have a name, but the story is fascinating. Abbas Effendi (this was 'Abdu'l-Bahá's actual name – Abdu'l-Baha is a title, meaning, 'Servant of Bahá'u'lláh') was made aware that a Christian merchant had taken advantage of one of the Bahá'ís who had purchased charcoal outside the city. When the merchant saw that it was better quality than he had been able to obtain, he confiscated it and offered no payment. The newly arrived Bahá'ís had little power to resist such actions.

Abbas Effendi had sent the Bahá'í to purchase the charcoal, so he went to the merchant's place of business and stood quietly by the door for some time. Not being noticed, he went in and sat down in silence for three hours. Finally, the merchant asked him if he was 'one of those prisoners that came here.' When 'Abdu'l-Bahá answered affirmatively, the merchant asked what they had done to deserve imprisonment. When 'Abdu'l-Bahá said: "We have done

---

[77] See Moojan Momen, *Bahá'u'lláh*. (Oxford, Oneworld, 2007, 95. Also: Taherzadeh. *The Revelation of Bahá'u'lláh*. (Oxford, Oneworld, 1983), vol.3, 221

nothing. We are persecuted as Christ was persecuted," the merchant responded: "What do you know of Christ?"

When the merchant discovered that 'Abdu'l-Bahá was familiar with the Bible and revered Christ, he became more interested, sat down and asked many questions, answers to which included interpretations of the New Testament that he had not heard before. They talked for two hours, the merchant returned the money and became a friend to 'Abdu'l-Bahá and their families were friends for many years, according to Bahiyyih Khanum, the daughter of Bahá'u'lláh, who tells this story. [78]

Winning the friendship of the populace of 'Akká was certainly not easy nor did it come quickly. They had been told that these 'Persians' were blasphemers and dangerous criminals. However, after a few years, this all changed, as people saw the true character and actions of the Bahá'ís and became acquainted with the person of Bahá'u'lláh.

As we mentioned earlier, many of the people of 'Akká credited Bahá'u'lláh's coming with a change in the nature of their city, some even saying that the climate had changed. And, of course, as we saw earlier, they remembered that Bahá'u'lláh was responsible for bringing fresh water to the city, something that every resident was grateful for every day of their lives.

A Physician
We know very little about this Irishman named Dr. Cormick, but what we know is quite interesting and he is a famous Christian

---

78 Ibid. p 113.

because he was the very first European Christian to encounter an early Bahá'í figure. As you have heard, the Bahá'í Faith was preceded by an earlier faith, the religion of the Báb. We have described this earlier and if you need a refresher, return to chapter one, where you can read about the early history of the Bahá'í Faith.

In fact, it was not called the Bahá'í Faith from the very beginning but rather it was called the Bábi Faith, after the religion founded by 'the Báb,' a title which means the 'Gate.' The Báb's central message was that very soon God would manifest Himself in a great messenger who would bring peace and unity to the entire world. Bahá'u'lláh was a follower of the Báb and in less than twenty years after the Báb made His announcement of God's plan to send a new messenger of His Presence and His Will, Bahá'u'lláh declared Himself to be that one that the Báb had predicted would soon arise, 'He whom God shall make manifest.'

In 1850, the Persian clergy and political figures conspired to put the Báb to death, a situation so similar to that of Christ. As the Báb was being held in a cell, Dr. Cormick was sent in to examine him, thus becoming the earliest known Christian contact with the new faith. We know nothing more, but Dr. Cormick, you are a 'famous Christian' to me, because you are the first and only European Christian to meet the Báb (other than two carpenters from Armenia – see below).[79]

When Dr. Cormick asked the Báb to explain something about His religion and indicated he might even be willing to adopt it, the Báb

---

[79] See *Dawnbreakers*, 320. This is an early history of the Faith, written by Nabil.

replied that He had no doubt that all Europeans would someday be His followers. When Dr. Cormick gave a report to the Shah which indicated he thought the Báb's life should be spared, the Báb (Who would later be executed) was spared, but was tortured (just as Christ was tortured prior to His death).

While torturing him, the Báb was accidentally struck in the face. He asked for the same Dr. Cormick He had seen before to provide treatment. Though Dr. Cormick did not learn anything of the Báb's 'doctrine,' he remarked that two Armenian carpenters (famous Christians?) had seen the Báb reading the Bible, which led Dr. Cormick to conclude that the Báb had what he called 'a certain approach to Christianity.'[80] It is worth noting that when the Báb sent out his disciples (they were called 'Letters of the Living'), he gave them a stirring and well-remembered speech which included some of the same words and phrases that Christ spoke to His disciples when He sent them out. Many observers, both Christian and Bahá'í, have noticed the striking similarity of the lives of the Báb and Christ.

---

80 See E. G Browne. *Materials for the Study of the Bábi Religion*. (Cambridge: University Press,1918), 261f.

CHAPTER 10

Two Army Captains, two Generals, some Monks and a Watchmaker. Plus, more on the first Christian to become a Bahá'í

§

AN ARMY CAPTAIN WITNESSES MARTYRDOMS

IN THE EMPLOY OF THE Shah of Iran was an Austrian officer, Captain van Goumoens, who saw the terrifying tortures and executions that accompanied martyrdoms of Bábís in the beginning days of the Faith. He finally had to tender his resignation as he could no longer witness such inhuman cruelty. His account, which was published back in Austria is more graphic that I wish to recount, but I will give you several sentences of a longer description: (Keep in mind that the Bahá'ís were called Bábis at an early point.)

"They will skin the soles of the Bábi's feet, soak the wounds in boiling oil, shoe the foot like the foot of a horse, and compel the victim to run...Put him out of his pain! No! The executioner swings the whip, and - I myself have had to witness it - the unhappy victim of hundredfold tortures runs!"

At the end of his lengthy description, Captain van Goumoens states: "When I read over again what I have written, I am overcome by the thought that those who are with you in our dearly beloved Austria may doubt the full truth of the picture, and accuse me of exaggeration. Would to God that I had not lived to see it! ...At present I never leave my house, in order not to meet with fresh scenes of horror." These depredations went on for months and over the remaining decades of the nineteenth century, with upwards of twenty thousand Bahá'ís being martyred for their Faith.

Ernst Renan, French philosopher and writer and expert on the middle-east, said that the terrifying massacre in Tihran, the capital city of Persia, represented what he called "a day perhaps unparalleled in the history of the world." (both quotes from Goumeons and Renan are from: Shoghi Effendi, *God Passes By*, 1944, 67-68) [81]

ANOTHER ARMY CAPTAIN

In chapter one above we told you of an army Captain named Sam Khan. Since you may not have read this chapter on Bahá'í History, let's repeat the information here. Sam Khan stands near the head of the rank of 'Famous Christians' in the Bahá'í story.

Just as Christ had a forerunner, Bahá'u'lláh also had One who went before Him. His name was 'The Báb (actually a title, meaning 'The Gate,' signifying that He was the gate through which the 'Promised One of all Ages' would walk.) The same thing happened to the Báb as happened to both John the Baptist and Jesus. The clergy and the state had the Báb executed on July 9, 1850.

---

[81] Captain van Goumeons account is lengthy and quite graphic, but details the horrific and unique tortures undergone by the followers of the Báb, thus explaining what would otherwise have been taken to be hyperbole by Renan.

An account of the apparently miraculous martyrdom of the Báb can be found in the *Encyclopedia Britannica*.[82] Look up this entire story in *The Dawnbreakers*, a history written by one of Bahá'u'lláh's disciples,[83] or have a Bahá'í friend tell it to you in detail because it is a fascinating historical moment, including a Christian Captain of the rifle forces who refused to carry out the Báb's final execution. His name was Sam Khan. (See bibliography for information and notation on *The Dawnbreakers*.)

Sam Khan was reluctant to carry out the execution. He told his soldiers that he feared the wrath of God, if he put to death a holy man (in addition to seeing the Báb as a godly man, he recognized from the Báb's green turban, that He was a descendant of Muhammad.) Sam Khan talked with the Báb, saying: "I profess the Christian Faith and entertain no ill will toward you. If your cause be the Cause of Truth, enable me to free myself from the obligation to shed your blood." The Báb replied*: **"Follow your instructions, and if your intention be sincere, the Almighty is surely able to relieve you of your perplexity."** (Cedarquist, *The Story of Bahá'u'lláh*, 2005, 82)

Perplexity it was, for on the one hand, he had an order from the highest level of government; on the other hand, he did not want to commit an unjust act against someone who was a descendant of the Prophet Mohammed and a person who said He brought a new message from God. Based on what the Báb had said, Sam Khan proceeded with the execution. The short version is this: After seven-hundred

---

82 Or, brittanica.com
83 Nabil-i-Azam. See bibliography for information on his book, *The Dawnbreakers*.

fifty rifles had been discharged and with dense smoke covering the entire courtyard, the Báb was nowhere to be found.

Moments later, the Báb was discovered back in his prison room, telling the executioners they could now proceed with their plan, as he had now finished his work on earth. Sam Khan promptly refused to go through with the final execution and another regiment was brought in who carried out the deed.

Sam Khan will always be remembered fondly and well by the Bahá'ís. His sincerity and desire to do justice gives credit to his Christian ideals and beliefs as well as his respect and tolerance for Islam. He is to the Bahá'ís a 'Famous Christian.'

A General

Unfortunately, again we don't have a name, just a fascinating story. Bahá'u'lláh, when in 'Akká, almost never granted interviews, except to those of His followers who had arduously journeyed from Iran to be in His Presence for just moments, or even to view Him from some distance, across a moat (this journey, from Iraq or Iran, was often on foot, over a period of several months). However, many leaders of thought, poets, intellectuals and religious leaders tried to gain an audience with Him. On one rare occasion, He did grant an interview with the Governor of 'Akká and a 'European General' who came with him.

As the Governor and the General crossed the threshold into the room where Bahá'u'lláh sat on a divan, the General simply 'melted' to the floor and remained silently on his knees throughout the time that Bahá'u'lláh and the Governor talked. Having worked for the military and having met a few generals, I can say with confidence and you can guess that this behavior is seldom seen with generals. So, I am asking, what happened in the case of the 'General Who Knelt by the Door'?[84]

All I can say is that different people had different reactions to Bahá'u'lláh, just as was the case with Jesus Christ. The General, somehow, realized or actually felt the Spiritual Presence of God that was represented in Bahá'u'lláh. He could not stand, or speak, but moved to a position and attitude of worship. Some Bahá'ís who came to visit Bahá'u'lláh on pilgrimage, found that they could not speak or even stand, and had this experience of moving to their knees (Some even laid themselves flat on the floor). This was understandable for them, but what of this 'European General'? Your guess is as good as mine. Is it not intriguing to speculate on what was going on in the General's mind and feelings?

Who was he? We do not know. But, for me, he is an unusual person, spiritually attuned and certainly a famous Christian in the Bahá'í story.

Intelligence Officer (who Became a Poet and Mystic)

Wellesley Tudor Pole (1884-1968) led a full life. From early in the twentieth century, riding with Lawrence of Arabia, capturing Jerusalem, fighting the Turks in northern Palestine in the First World War, he went on to become poet, philosopher, writer and mystic and one of the most well-known Englishmen of his time. In addition to all of this, he had, in 1908 and 1910, met and greatly admired

---

84 Shoghi Effendi. *God Passes By*. (Wilmette, IL: Bahá'í Publishing Trust, 1944), 192.

'Abdu'l-Bahá. In the next decade, he was serving as an intelligence officer in the British Army, as they fought the Turks in Palestine.

After helping liberate Jerusalem, he discovered that: "The Turkish line will probably run through Haifa shortly [this is where 'Abdu'l-Bahá lived at the time]. The Bahá'í leader and his family are in imminent danger and at the moment, of course, we are powerless. His position and prestige is not understood among the Authorities here. It is not even realized that he controls a remarkable religious movement, wholly devoid of political and military associations; which can number many millions of adherents throughout the Near and Middle-East. Jews, Muslims of various sects, Christians, Parsis, Hindoos, Kurds unite under the Bahá'í banner of Spiritual Fellowship.

Wellesley Tudor Pole

"May not these people [the Bahá'ís] contribute much, later, to the harmonizing of Sectarian and Oriental Religious feuds? Is it too much to ask the Authorities at home to request the Authorities here to afford every protection and consideration?" (Letter from TP to Sir Mark Sykes, M.P. [so to speak, his 'Congressman'], 24-12-17, in File 23353/W/44: Foreign Office 371 3396) [85] More, in a moment, as to why he is a famous Christian in the Bahá'í story.[86]

ANOTHER GENERAL: After the ascension of Bahá'u'lláh in 1892, the cities of 'Akká and Haifa were still in the hands of Syria. In the years prior to World War I there was great ferment in that area. When the war began, very well-known British General Edmund Allenby had captured Jerusalem from the Turks in 1917. By 1918 Jamal Pasha, a commander of the Turkish Army who was still in control in the 'Akká area, had threatened to 'crucify'[87] 'Abdu'l-Bahá and his family, so Bahá'ís in Britain and the United States were alarmed. ('Abdu'l-Bahá had been knighted by the British several years earlier, for services rendered during a famine, so this may have made him a target for hatred by the Turks, who were on the German side in the war).

The Bahá'ís of Britain, however, were the ones most likely to be able to influence the situation, since Britain held a mandate over what was then called 'Palestine.' Bahá'ís such as Lady Blomfield of Britain (who had visited 'Abdu'l-Bahá earlier in a pilgrimage) were

---

85 Copy of this letter at: http://dimensionsbeyond.typepad.com/dimensions-beyond/wellesley-tudor-pole/ A section at this site is titled: "A Tale of Life, Death and Armageddon: The Rescue of 'Abdu'l-Baha."
86 wikipedia.com appears to be an excellent source for information on Wellesley Tudor Pole. He is a fascinating character.
87 This means *literally* what it says. Jamal Pasha was cruel and known to be ready to punish harshly.

able to work through their husbands, who were 'Lords' of the British Empire and further through them to reach the Prime Minister and Foreign Secretary Lord Balfour.[88] Balfour and General Allenby had been informed by an intelligence officer at the front of the battle, Major Tudor Pole, that 'Abdu'l-Bahá was, indeed, in danger. We have already heard above what Major Tudor Pole stated about the danger to 'Abdu'l-Bahá.

Sara Louisa Lady Blomfield

Though it is speculation, Allenby would not have changed his battle plans, unless contacted by the Prime Minister. Balfour then sends a direct cable to General Allenby to do whatever is necessary to protect 'Abdu'l-Bahá. The story is too lengthy to tell here, but General Allenby actually changes his war plans and marches on

---

88 Yes, this is *the* Lord Balfour, who wrote the Balfour Declaration in 1917 to Baron Rothschild, without which the establishment of the nation of Israel would have been doubtful or much more difficult.

Haifa, where 'Abdu'l-Bahá is living and takes deliberate steps to protect him. For this, I call General Allenby a famous Christian.[89]

So much depended on the leadership of the Bahá'í Faith by 'Abdu'l-Bahá at this time. Bahá'u'lláh made it clear in His written will that after His death, all Bahá'ís must follow the leadership of 'Abdu'l-Bahá. The Bahá'í world therefore owes a great debt to this general and, by the way, to Major Tudor Pole (he knew quite a bit about the Bahá'í Faith), who played his own part as a famous Christian. Major Pole also wrote: "What is the special appeal voiced by Bahá'u'lláh and his son, which has resulted in so many of their followers the world over asserting that they are no longer Jews, Christians, Muslims or Buddhists, as such but have become Bahá'ís? The answer may well be that as each religious revelation becomes crystallized, dogmatic and formal, the need arises for Truth to be restated in terms that conform to the needs of the new hour." [90] (The Silent Road, 1960 p. 143) [91]

The Bahá'ís were, indeed, grateful to General Allenby but especially to Major Tudor Pole. The British National Spiritual Assembly said that the abiding place of Major Tudor Pole would rest on the part he played during 1918 in helping to save the life of 'Abdu'l-Bahá. As a 'sidebar' to this discussion, General Allenby was only able to march

---

89 See: Tudor Pole. *Writing on the Ground*. (London: Neville Spearman, 1968), 153. See footnote 91 for access to this out of print book.
90 bahaitributes.wordpress.com
91 Both *The Silent Road* and *Writing on the Ground* are no longer in print. However, here is a site for a PDF of both books in their entirety (good reads): http://bahai-library.com/author/Wellesley%20Tudor+Pole

on Haifa after winning a battle at Megiddo (guess what the Biblical name for Megiddo is: Armageddon). [92]

SOME CHRISTIAN MONKS AND A MOUNTAINTOP MONASTERY

As stated, Bahá'u'lláh was allowed, in later years to visit from 'Akká to nearby Haifa, where He always went to Mt. Carmel. (He was still formally under 'house arrest,' though it had been partially relaxed toward the end of His life). The city of Haifa is at the foot of Carmel, the Old Testament 'Mountain of the Lord,' associated with Elijah. The mountain is just several hours west of Jesus's birthplace of Nazareth, in the district of Galilee (which is why Jesus has often been referred to as 'The Galilean.')

On a visit to Mt. Carmel, Bahá'u'lláh and His followers visited a monastery of Carmelite monks and signed their guest book. The monks offered shelter for the night, but He demurred. Outside and a little ways away, He pitched a tent and revealed one of the most important Tablets of His entire ministry, 'The Tablet of Carmel' (referring to the Mountain of Carmel). In it, with the 'Voice of God' doing the speaking, we hear:

"All Glory be to this Day, the Day in which the fragrance of mercy have been wafted over all created things, a Day so blest that past ages and centuries can never hope to rival it, a Day which the countenance of the Ancient of Days hath turned toward His holy seat. Thereupon, the voices of all created things, and beyond them, those

---

[92] wikipedia.org gives good treatment for Viscount Allenby with pictures and a statement about his victory at Meggido.

of the Concourse on High, were heard calling aloud: 'Haste thee, O Carmel for lo, the light of the Countenance of God, the Ruler of the Kingdom of Names and Fashioner of the Heavens, hath been lifted up upon thee...Call out to Zion, O Carmel, and announce the joyful tidings: He that was hidden from mortal eyes is come...ere long will God sail His Ark on thee, and will manifest the people of Baha who have been mentioned in the Book of Names.'" (Momen, *Bahá'u'lláh*, 2007, 189-90)

QUESTION: Earlier, I told you that it made me uncomfortable for Bahá'u'lláh to say He was 'the Father.' Now, I have that same uneasy feeling about Bahá'u'lláh associating Himself with 'The Ancient of Days,' clearly a name for God!

RESPONSE: And I responded to your previous comment by pointing out that Bahá'u'lláh and Christ said *both* that they were not God *and* that to see them was to see God. This is fully explained, with the proper New Testament quotes in my earlier book *Questions from Christians*. Christ clearly said that to see Him was to see God, but He also said He was not God. Once, when one of His disciples called Him 'good,' He replied: **"Why do you call me good?"** Jesus answered. **"No one is good--except God alone."** (Mark 10:18). Christians, I realize, have usually resolved this apparent contradiction using the doctrine of the Trinity.

Bahá'ís, on the other hand, don't see a dilemma or contradiction here. We see both statements as true. When Bahá'u'lláh or Christ say that to see them is to see God, we accept that the fullness of God's Presence is 'in' the Manifestation of God represented by one who appears among us as a human being. When they say, as both did, that they are not God (Bahá'u'lláh said this very clearly, too) this is their statement that there is only one God, who nevertheless appears from time to time in human history in what Bahá'u'lláh called **"the human temple."** As we said before, Christians needed the doctrine of Trinity (devised hundreds of years after the New Testament was written) because of their understanding of God's Presence as 'Incarnation,' while Bahá'ís derive their understanding from Bahá'u'lláh's explanation of 'Manifestation.'

While these two explanations of God's Presence in history, 'Incarnation' and 'Manifestation' often seem so different, or at odds, both of them are statements attempting to explain what appears to be a fact of history: that God thrusts His Power and full Presence into human affairs from time to time, causing the 'Word of God' to appear in a 'human temple.'

The same discomfort you feel was exactly how I felt when I first heard statements of this kind. I then realized, though, that this uneasiness was the same type of feeling that Jewish listeners had when Christ said He would forgive sins (something they believed only God could do) or that he was 'sitting at the right hand of God' or that 'the Father and I are one.' These statements sounded directly false and blasphemous to Jewish ears. Perhaps this is why so few Jews became His followers.

But some did! Among them, Matthew, Mark, John, Peter and the Pharisee and Roman Citizen Saul of Tarsus, who later became the Apostle Paul.

In my case, I had to pray and read and pray some more and talk with Bahá'ís to begin to understand what Bahá'u'lláh meant by the statements above in the Tablet of Carmel, just as Jews who became followers of Jesus had to pray, think and pray some more to understand who He was. They finally were able to give their lives to the One Who called Himself the 'Son of Man' and Who was seen by His followers (and by Bahá'ís) as the 'Son of God.' And, I was finally able to give my life, which had already been given to the Son… to give my life again, to the 'Father of all Mankind.'

Oh, and as to the comment of the 'Voice of God' that someday God would **'*sail His Ark*'** on the mountain. This is an obvious reference to Noah's Ark and the safety that it brought, symbolically, to humanity. In this case, it is also a 'play on words,' where Ark (like Noah's) is like Arc, the Arc of buildings that are laid out halfway up the mountain of Carmel, buildings that make up the administrative center of the Bahá'í Faith, often referred to as 'the World Center.'

These buildings and monuments truly do form an Arc that spreads a quarter of a kilometer across the brow of the mountain, comprising the Shrine of the Báb, the Center for the Study of the Texts, the Archives Building, the International Teaching Center, (soon to be added will be an International Library) and finally, most importantly, the Seat of the Universal House of Justice, the highest administrative institution of the Bahá'í Faith, a body envisioned and described by Bahá'u'lláh Himself.[93]

---

[93] Not a part of the Arc, but some distance away, a House of Worship will someday be constructed, very near to the 'Cave of Elijah' on the southern brow of the Mountain of Carmel.

Do you remember the 'woman at the well' and the 'Canaanite woman' who encountered Jesus that we spoke of earlier? I speculated that they may have experienced a life change because they met and talked with Jesus. We do not know, but I for one think they experienced a transformation of spirit and outlook. (In my days as a student minister, I preached a sermon on this topic). As for these Carmelite monks, did one or several of them experience a changed, transformed life because they met Bahá'u'lláh or heard Him Revealing the Word of God?

When Bahá'u'lláh earlier wrote a letter to all the Christians of the world, He addressed the 'monks' of the world, saying: *"O concourse of monks! If ye choose to follow Me, I will make you heirs of My Kingdom; and if ye transgress against Me, I will, in My long-suffering, endure it patiently, and I, verily, am the Ever-Forgiving, the All-Merciful.*

"O land of Syria! [Mt. Carmel was then located in the country of Syria] *What hath become of thy righteousness? Thou art, in truth, ennobled by the footsteps of thy Lord. Hast thou perceived the fragrance of heavenly reunion, or art thou to be accounted of the heedless?* (Bahá'u'lláh, *Tablets of Bahá'u'lláh*, 1978, 14)

After Bahá'u'lláh left the monastery, when the monks heard the beautiful and sonorous voice of Bahá'u'lláh revealing the 'Tablet of Carmel,' were they curious about what it meant? Did they inquire? Did they experience 'wonder'? They were so close to the 'Father of all Mankind.' I like to think that at least one of them became more aware of the Spirit of God Who been in their midst and experienced a deepened, changed life as a result, just as I like to think that the woman at the well and the Canaanite woman were changed by their experience of being close to 'the Son of God.' What do you think? [94]

A Watchmaker (And More about the First Christian to Become a Follower of Bahá'u'lláh)

There are two parts to this story. The first part deals with Constantine, the Watchmaker, who apparently knew someone at a prison in Alexandria, Egypt. We will get back to Constantine later. Many people are in this prison, but the two in which we are interested are a man named Nabil-i-Azam and another named Faris. Nabil is very well-known and even legendary in Bahá'í history, mainly for writing the book *Dawnbreakers*, which describes the early history of the Faith, telling the dramatic story of the Báb and His disciples, who were called 'The Letters of the Living.'

Nabil is also known as a faithful and productive disciple of Bahá'u'lláh. In fact, he was in this prison for this reason: Bahá'u'lláh had sent him on a mission to Cairo in May, 1868 to help and assist another disciple who was in prison in Khartoum. Instead of being able to help, he himself wound up in prison in Alexandria.

With him in the same cell, is a Syrian physician named Faris, a Christian who had been thrown into prison for financial reasons. With little knowledge of who Nabil is, and knowing nothing about the Bahá'í Faith (including the fact that Bahá'ís revere Christ as a Manifestation of God), Faris sets about the task of converting Nabil,

---

94 wikipedia has a full treatment of the Stella Maris monastery on Mt. Carmel (Elijah's cave is nearby). These Monks, who originally were hermits inhabiting the cave of Elijah, have been in this spot since the Crusades in the twelfth century.

who he probably thinks is Muslim, to the Christian Faith. Nabil listens thoughtfully and respectfully and when Faris has, so to speak, spent his argument, Nabil begins to tell him about Bahá'u'lláh, the 'Promise of all Ages,' and points out to him that Bahá'u'lláh is the Return of the Spirit of Christ.

We can imagine that Faris resists this interpretation, but finally, Nabil, who has been around Bahá'u'lláh for many years and is 'on fire' with faith, manages to bring Faris into strong discipleship as a follower of Bahá'u'lláh. You will see how strongly shortly. Nabil has a dream one night, in which Bahá'u'lláh informs him that in eighty-one days he will 'have reason to rejoice.' Exactly eighty-one days later, the following happened.

Nabil and Faris are on the rooftop of the prison. Prisoners were apparently allowed there to escape the heat of the prison. From there they could see out into the Mediterranean and could also look down into the city street. It is the eighty-first day and Nabil is not someone to ignore this type of dream, so he is expecting something to happen. It does! He looks down into the street and, shockingly, sees a Persian man he knows, by the name of Muhammad Ibrahim, who had in the past been the cook for Bahá'u'lláh and His family and large group of followers (around seventy people).

He calls down to Muhammad, who is as surprised as Nabil is to see him. Muhammad informs Nabil that, in fact, Bahá'u'lláh is on an Austrian Lloyd steamer that can be seen in the harbor by the prisoners. He explains that Bahá'u'lláh is being further banished from Edirne to 'Akká, Syria (now Israel), the fearful and frightening prison city.

He then says he is in the city to buy provisions for Bahá'u'lláh's family and group of followers who are on the ship. He is able to come into the prison to visit his friend and both Faris and Nabil become excited about Bahá'u'lláh being so near. Faris has just accepted Bahá'u'lláh as his Lord and is frustrated, as is Nabil, at being so close, but at the same time, so far away. The prison is near the harbor, so they can see the ship. It is only hundreds of yards away. The sight of it is both gratifying and painful at the same time.

They cannot sleep that night. Both of them write letters to Bahá'u'lláh and they ask a young Christian man named Constantine the Watchmaker to deliver them. The next morning, they watch Constantine in a small boat, rowing toward the steamer. Then disaster strikes: With Constantine having not yet reached the steamer, the ship now begins to move away!

Faris and Nabil wail, then fall to their knees in prayer. They cannot bear to look at this tragedy. So close, but so far! When they look up, they cannot believe their eyes. The large ship slows, then stops. They do not know why. Both Christians and Bahá'ís have witnessed historical happenings that have an element of mystery and suspected divine intervention. Whatever you and I may think, I can assure you that Nabil thought that God had a hand in slowing the ship.

The row boat with Constantine catches up and Constantine boards the steamer and the letters are delivered to Bahá'u'lláh, who reads Faris' letter to His family and companions. Bahá'u'lláh pens a reply to both Faris and to Nabil, which Constantine brings back.

Constantine is excited and awestruck and tells them: "By God, I have seen the face of the Heavenly Father." [95]

In later years, Bahá'u'lláh several times revealed Tablets which mention this famous Christian and Faris is believed to be the first Christian to believe in Bahá'u'lláh. Bahá'u'lláh was so happy in receiving this letter of declaration of Faith from Faris, that He asked that copies of Faris' letter be sent to the Bahá'ís of Persia. Some scholars believe (though it cannot be proved, at this time) that the 'Letter to the Christians' which you will read at the end of this book, was written in honor of Faris. The following are just a few of the comments in Faris' letter to Bahá'u'lláh.

"O Thou the Glory of the Most Glorious and the Exalted of the Most Exalted! I write this letter and present it to the One who has been subjected to the same sufferings as Jesus Christ…it is incumbent upon us to offer praise and thanksgiving…O Thou who hast endured for our sake sufferings and tribulations. Strengthen our faith, choose us for Thy service and accept us as martyrs in Thy path so that our blood may be shed for the love of Thee. We are weak and ignorant, confer upon us Thy glory so that we may not be among the losers.

"Grant us the distinction of love and faith, and cleanse our hearts from whatsoever runs counter to Thy good pleasure. Aid us to forget our own selves so that we may seek no rest in Thy service except by Thy leave and pleasure. [Author's Note: In the following

---

95 For information on Constantine, see Adib Taherzadeh. *The Revelation of Bahá'u'lláh*. (Oxford: Ronald, 1983), vol.3, p. 4.

paragraph, Faris writes poetically, as one can more freely and easily do in Arabic, and addresses the ship that Bahá'u'lláh is on, the sea on which the ship steams, the city of Alexandria, which is the city being left, and the prison-city of 'Akká, Bahá'u'lláh's destination]

"O Thou who knowest the secrets of the hearts! Art Thou sailing in an ark made of wood? O how I long to be a part of that vessel, for it is blessed to be a carrier of the Lord. O, the surging sea! Is thy restlessness because of the fear of the glorious Lord? O Alexandria! art thou grief-stricken because He who is the Ever-living, the All-wise, is leaving thy shores? O, the desolate city of 'Akká! Thou art clapping thy hands in fervent joy and art in a state of rapture and ecstasy, for the Lord in His great glory will bless thy land with His footsteps..." (Taherzadeh, *The Revelation of Bahá'u'lláh* vol. 3, 1983, 6-9)

As for Constantine the Watchmaker and, for that matter, as for Faris, both famous Christians, we have no more solid information about them whatever. But here again, like the woman at the well and the Canaanite woman, who met Jesus, we can hope and believe that both Constantine and Faris led changed lives after interacting with the One that they saw, in the case of Constantine, as 'the Father' and in the case of Faris, as his newly-found 'Lord,' the Returned Christ and 'The Father of All Mankind.' [96]

We have some indication that Faris returned to Syria to teach the good news of the appearance of Bahá'u'lláh, but this is uncertain. We hope someday to uncover the trace of Faris, the first Christian to

---

[96] Unfortunately, we have not yet located a copy of the letter Bahá'u'lláh wrote to Faris. Hopefully, the letter and other details about Faris will surface.

become a Bahá'í. Until then he is certainly, for us, a famous Christian in the Bahá'í story. And, we have the word of Bahá'u'lláh, as told to us by author and historian Adib Taherzadeh, that Bahá'u'lláh said in a Tablet (speaking of Faris) "God transformed his heart and created him anew." [These are Taherzadeh's words, but faithfully reporting what he read in this unpublished Tablet.] (Taherzadeh, *The Revelation of Bahá'u'lláh*, vol. 3, p. 9)

QUESTION: Well, I remember what you said about Bahá'u'lláh being in prison, comparing the situation with Christ, who was arrested, tortured and executed for so-called crimes, but I'm left wondering about this Nabil you have told me about. If he is so great and you called him 'well-known and legendary' in Bahá'í history,' then why was he in prison? It seems lots of the early Bábis and Bahá'ís were in prison. If so, why should we think positively about them? Were they criminals?

RESPONSE: When a new religion starts, when a new Revelation from God appears on the scene, two groups are upset: The clergy of the existing religion and the current political leaders, both of whom fear that their power will be challenged by the new religion. So, what do they do? They persecute, torture and execute those who believe in this new 'dangerous' religion. And, in any case, they throw them into jail.

We need to remember that the Apostle Paul was thrown into prison, as was St. Peter and others from early in the Christian dispensation. St. Stephen was stoned to death for the crime of 'blasphemy' (with persecutor Saul watching, not yet transformed into St. Paul). Christians were arrested, tortured and put to death for several centuries, with false accusations of criminal activity. Why? Because existing regimes saw them as threatening to the established order.

Apparently, as Christians know so well, being in jail is an ordinary experience if you are an early believer in a new religion. (Think Peter and Paul and others.) It has been no different in the Bahá'í story. Bahá'ís are still arrested, and jailed in Iran, for no other reason than their faith in Bahá'u'lláh. Over the last four decades, Baha'is have faced government harassment, persecution, imprisonments and executions. This continues through the early part of the 21st Century. [97]

---

[97] For this incident at Alexandria and for information of Faris Effendi, Nabil and Constantine, see Adib Taherzadeh. *The Revelation of Bahá'u'lláh* (Oxford: Ronald, 1983), vol. 3, pp 6-9.

CHAPTER 11

The Christian who saved the life of Bahá'u'lláh and the Christian who gave his life so that Bahá'u'lláh might live Plus: Bahá'u'lláh wrote a letter to you!

THE CHRISTIAN WHO SAVED BAHÁ'U'LLÁH'S LIFE

YES, THERE IS A CHRISTIAN whose action almost certainly saved Bahá'u'lláh's life. Here is the scene. Only a few years after the Báb announced His mission, namely, to let the world know that God was about to reveal Himself in a Manifestation that the Báb simply called, "Him Whom God shall make manifest." As you've heard already, Bahá'u'lláh, Who was one of the Báb's disciples, revealed Himself less than two decades later as that Manifestation, and told the world that He, as 'the Father of all mankind' had come to bring to the entire world an era of unity and peace.

But before Bahá'u'lláh revealed Himself, Persia was aflame with the fact that two young Bábis had attempted to assassinate the Shah. Such actions were totally against the will of Bahá'u'lláh. They did not succeed, but what did happen was that the government and the populace turned against the followers of the Báb with vengeance. This was part, but only a part, of the reason for the many martyrdoms of Bábis of that period. Even before this, and after as well, Bábis and later Bahá'ís were martyred solely because of their belief in Bahá'u'lláh.

Since Bahá'u'lláh was a follower of the Báb, he and others were under suspicion and thrown into prison, an unlighted, underground area, (used in earlier years as a bathhouse) known as the 'Black Pit.' So, Bahá'u'lláh and a number of others (about 30) are in this terrifying prison, in heavy chains. From time to time, the jailer comes into the 'pit' and announces a name. That person, after being embraced by Bahá'u'lláh and his other friends, goes to his execution. The jailers and executioners are puzzled as, often, the condemned man goes to his death singing and dancing. This 'lottery of death' goes on over the four months that Bahá'u'lláh and His companions lie in the damp, dark, filthy prison.

Before I tell you why Bahá'u'lláh did not suffer execution at that time, I want to challenge you with a weird riddle: What possible connection can there be between the famous nineteenth century stories from American literature, such as 'The Legend of Sleepy Hollow' and 'Rip Van Winkle' on the one hand and the story of Bahá'u'lláh's imprisonment in the 'Black Pit?'

Before you think I have lost my mind or my way, consider this: The writer of those stories was Washington Irving, who was the United States Ambassador to Spain in 1842-46. While he was there he made a friend of Russian Prince Dolgorukov, who was also in the diplomatic corps. Together they explored the confluence of Islam and Christianity that had occurred in Spain. Irving had even written a biography of Muhammad. And, as it turns out, this same Dolgorukov was the Russian Minister at the Russian Legation in Teheran, Iran from 1845 to 1854. The date of Bahá'u'lláh's imprisonment in the 'Black Pit' is August through December of 1852.

Bahá'u'lláh had a brother-in-law Mirza Majid Ahi, who was a secretary at the Russian Legation. He apparently influenced Dolgorukov to speak to the Court of the Shah, asking that Bahá'u'lláh's life be spared, even offering to arrange for Him to be taken into protective exile in Russia, which Bahá'u'lláh declined. Some people who have investigated this feel that Dolgorukov gave veiled threats to the Court saying that the Russian Crown would be highly displeased if harm came to Bahá'u'lláh.

Some people believe that Dolgorukov went 'out on a limb' to say this in the Shah's Court, not having had time to consult with his diplomatic superiors. He was taking a great risk, if so. But Bahá'u'lláh tells us that his superior, the Russian Ambassador had become interested in his case and had even requested a copy of Bahá'u'lláh's 'Most Holy Book.'[98] This may have happened later than Dolgorukov's intervention, but it unlikely that it is coincidental that the intercession by this member of the Russian Embassy would not be connected in some way to the Ambassador's request to Baha'u'llah. Why Dolgorukov's intervention was so successful was that Iran was very concerned about possible war with Russia, who had already shown willingness to seize part of Iran's territory.

---

98 Bahá'u'lláh's statement on this is fully covered in the letter to his disciple, Ali Haydar. See *Andalib,*, vol. 16,, no. 64 [Fall, 1997]: 4-7. This Ambassador (name unknown) is a 'famous Christian,' since He was the first Christian to request and receive a copy of Bahá'u'lláh's 'Most Holy Book,' more than one-hundred years before it was translated into English and one hundred-thirty years before it was released in publication in the 'Western' world for Western Bahá'ís and Christians to read. Earlier, there had been an Arabic version published in the early 1890's in India, and Arabic and Farsi (Persian) versions in the Middle East.

Bahá'u'lláh testifies to the effectiveness of this minister in a personal letter to one of His followers (Ali Haydar): *"In the Tablets to the Kings a mention was revealed of this wronged one's imprisonment and the protection afforded by the resident minister of the glorious Russian state, may God aid him. O Tsar, one of your ambassadors helped me when I was in prison, weighed down by manacles and chains. Therefore, God has inscribed for you a station that no one can know. Beware lest you exchange this august station. During the days when this wronged one was being tormented in the dungeon, the ambassador of that glorious state--may God assist him-- arose with perfect zeal to rescue me."* (*Andalib*, vol. 16, no. 64 [Fall, 1997]: 4-7)

As mentioned above, it is clear that Bahá'u'lláh was in danger of execution when this famous Christian intervened to save His life.[99] The government finally agreed that He be released from prison and allowed to go into exile in neighboring Iraq. After a month's recuperation, Bahá'u'lláh and His family and some followers departed for Baghdad and lifelong exile from their native country. [100]

The Christian who Gave his Life to Save the Life of Bahá'u'lláh

You will realize, I believe, that we have saved the best story of a 'famous Christian' until now. Yes, there is a Christian who chose to give up his

---

99 For information on Dolgorukov, see bahai-library.com/momen_encyclopedia_russia. This will also give you some other interesting information of the history of the Bahá'í Faith in Russia.

100 Bahá'u'lláh was fully cleared of all charges in the assassination attempt on the life of the Shah.

life so that Bahá'u'lláh could live. This is not my opinion. We have the word of Bahá'u'lláh for proof of this sacrifice, as you will hear.

Again, we must return to the city of Adrianople, modern Edirne, Turkey, where Bahá'u'lláh had been further exiled, after leaving Constantinople, modern Istanbul. These five years in Edirne had been difficult for everyone, certainly for Bahá'u'lláh. The difficulty culminated with Bahá'u'lláh's half-brother rebelling fully against Him. The half-brother had been jealous of Bahá'u'lláh all along, but now he spoke out strongly against Bahá'u'lláh and more, he engaged in acts that endangered the lives of Bahá'u'lláh and his family. Finally, he actually attempted to murder Bahá'u'lláh by poisoning Him. As a result of this deed, Bahá'u'lláh was near death, his case having been pronounced "hopeless."

Local doctors were called in, none of whom could think how to save Him and offered no hope for His recovery. Finally, the family called in a Doctor Shishman, from nearby Bulgaria. [Author's Note: When I first heard of Dr. Shishman, I thought that his name might signify that he was Jewish, but later I was informed by a Bulgarian Bahá'í that Shishman was a Christian] So, Dr. Shishman comes into the room of Bahá'u'lláh and is so alarmed at Bahá'u'lláh's condition that he immediately proclaims that he can do nothing for Him and there is no hope for recovery.

Then something remarkable happens. Dr. Shishman falls to the floor and has to be taken home. After making out a will and giving the name of another doctor to be called if needed, he dies four days later. Better get ready for this one! Bahá'u'lláh says that Dr. Shishman sacrificed his life so that Bahá'u'lláh could live. And, within several weeks, Bahá'u'lláh recovers. I guess that any person with a Christian background reading this thinks immediately of Christ's saying *"Greater love has no one than this, that he lay down his life for his friends."* (Jn 15:13

Before Shishman dies, Bahá'u'lláh is improving, though still not fully recovered. He is uneasy about Dr. Shishman. As a Manifestation of God, with divine knowledge, He may have been well-aware of the sacrifice of Shishman and concerned about him. Bahá'u'lláh sent his secretary, a man named Mirza Aqa Jan to Dr. Shishman's house. Now it was Shishman who was clearly dying. Shishman told Mirza Aqa Jan that "my prayers have been answered." So, this man is dying and he says "my prayers have been answered." And now, I ask you, what do you think Shishman's prayer was?

Bahá'u'lláh on several occasions intimated to friends and followers that Shishman sacrificed his life that Bahá'u'lláh might live.

Here is my question about the incident of Dr. Shishman: What did Shishman see that led him to make this sacrifice? If Dr. Shishman was a spiritually deep person, he may have been permitted to see exactly Who Bahá'u'lláh was. Additionally he may have realized that he was looking at Jesus Christ, in Spiritual Return. At that point, based upon seeing the One that Bahá'ís believe to be 'the Father of all Mankind' lying on his deathbed, Shishman had a choice to make, a choice that would not likely have occurred to him had he not fully realized Who and What Bahá'u'lláh was. [101]

---

101 For a citation on Shishman, see Shoghi Effendi, *God Passes By*, 1944, p 165.

Could Shishman, having made this startling discovery, this realization, just forget about it, turn around and go home? I think he could not do so and he made an instant and immediate decision to sacrifice his life with a prayer that Bahá'u'lláh would thereby be allowed to live. At least, this interpretation would make sense of his comment "my prayers have been answered." What was that prayer? We do not know, but my best guess is that he prayed that his own life be sacrificed as a ransom for the life of Bahá'u'lláh. What do you think?

§

This ends the catalogue of 'famous Christians' who played some part for good or for ill in the Bahá'í story. I hope you have enjoyed the telling of how so many Christians contributed some part of their lives, their fortune, and their influence in the direction of the development and unfolding of the world's newest religion - the Bahá'í Faith. Now that we think about it, there were quite a few 'famous Jews' who helped start the Christian religion. Above all, I believe that you and I will not be able to forget the dramatic story of that especially 'famous Christian,' Dr. Shishman of Bulgaria and his memorable and unusual sacrifice. But, before we end completely, let me say that the following chapter of this story is a letter that I maintain was written…to you!

CHAPTER 12

'Letter to the Christians.' A letter that Bahá'u'lláh wrote to all Christians and therefore: To You

§

QUESTION: Aren't you 'hyping' this a little?

RESPONSE: Well, I'm not trying to be overly dramatic, but I told you earlier that Bahá'u'lláh wrote a letter to all the Christians of the world, and therefore, I say, *to you!* So, what I think is that you join the ranks of 'famous Christians' in the Bahá'í story. He had already written to the Pope, to monks and to bishops. He had written to kings and a queen.

This letter, by contrast, is mostly for ordinary, everyday followers of Jesus. Its exact title is 'The Most Holy Tablet,' though it is usually called: 'Letter to the Christians.' Here it is with only a few clarifications [in brackets] where absolutely needed for full understanding.

"This is the Most Holy Tablet sent down from the holy kingdom unto the one[102] *who hath set his face towards the Object of the ado-*

---

102 This refers to the unknown Christian to whom this letter was written, apparently someone who recently declared their faith in Bahá'u'lláh. Or, (we speculate here), was it written to that 'Famous Christian,' Faris Effendi? Bahá'í scholar Taherzadeh lends his name to this speculation, while clearly labeling it as such.

ration of the world, He Who hath come from the heaven of eternity, invested with transcendent glory.

"In the name of the Lord, the Lord of great glory. This is an Epistle from Our presence unto him whom the veils of names have failed to keep back from God, the Creator of earth and heaven, that his eyes may be cheered in the days of his Lord, the Help in Peril, the Self-Subsisting.

"*Say, O followers of the Son!* [Bahá'u'lláh often calls Christians 'Followers of the Son' or 'Followers of the Spirit.'] **Have ye shut out yourselves from Me by reason of My Name? Wherefore ponder ye not in your hearts? Day and night ye have been calling upon your Lord, the Omnipotent, but when He came from the heaven of eternity in His great glory, ye turned aside from Him and remained sunk in heedlessness.**

"**Consider those who rejected the Spirit** [that is, Jesus] **when He came unto them with manifest dominion. How numerous the Pharisees who had secluded themselves in synagogues in His name, lamenting over their separation from Him, and yet when the portals of reunion were flung open and the divine Luminary shone resplendent from the Dayspring of Beauty, they disbelieved in God, the Exalted, the Mighty. They failed to attain His presence, notwithstanding that His advent had been promised them in the Book of Isaiah as well as in the Books of the Prophets and the Messengers.**

"**No one from among them turned his face towards the Dayspring of divine bounty except such as were destitute of any** *power amongst men. And yet, today, every man endowed with power and invested with sovereignty prideth himself on His Name. Moreover, call thou to mind the one who sentenced Jesus to death. He was the most learned of his age in his own country, whilst he who was only a fisherman believed in Him. Take good heed and be of them that observe the warning.*

"Consider likewise, how numerous at this time are the monks who have secluded themselves in their churches, calling upon the Spirit, [that is, Jesus] *but when He appeared through the power of Truth, they failed to draw nigh unto Him and are numbered with those that have gone far astray. Happy are they that have abandoned them and set their faces towards Him Who is the Desire of all that are in the heavens and all that are on the earth.*

"They read the Evangel [the New Testament] *and yet refuse to acknowledge the All-Glorious Lord, notwithstanding that He hath come through the potency of His exalted, His mighty and gracious dominion. We, verily, have come for your sakes, and have borne the misfortunes of the world for your salvation. Flee ye the One Who hath sacrificed His life that ye may be quickened? Fear God, O followers of the Spirit, and walk not in the footsteps of every divine that hath gone far astray. Do ye imagine that He seeketh His own interests, when He hath, at all times, been threatened by the swords of the enemies; or that He seeketh the vanities of the world, after He hath been imprisoned in the most desolate of cities? Be fair in your judgement and follow not the footsteps of the unjust.*

"Open the doors of your hearts. He Who is the Spirit [103] *verily standeth before them. Wherefore banish ye Him Who hath purposed to draw you nigh unto a Resplendent Spot? Say: We, in truth, have opened unto you the gates of the Kingdom. Will ye bar the doors of your houses in My face? This indeed is naught but a grievous error. He, verily, hath again come down from heaven, even as He came down from it the first time. Beware lest ye dispute that which He proclaimeth, even as the people before you disputed His utterances. Thus instructeth you the True One, could ye but perceive it.*

"The river Jordan is joined to the Most Great Ocean, and the Son, [Jesus] *in the holy vale, crieth out: 'Here am I, here am I O Lord, my God!', whilst Sinai circleth round the House, and the Burning Bush calleth aloud: 'He Who is the Desired One is come in His transcendent majesty.' Say, Lo! The Father is come, and that which ye were promised in the Kingdom is fulfilled! This is the Word which the Son concealed, when to those around Him He said: 'Ye cannot bear it now.' And when the appointed time was fulfilled and the Hour had struck, the Word shone forth above the horizon of the Will of God.*

"Beware, O followers of the Son, that ye cast it not behind your backs. Take ye fast hold of it. Better is this for you than all that ye possess. Verily He is nigh unto them that do good. The Hour which

---

103 Bahá'u'lláh here uses 'the Spirit,' which he most often uses to refer to Jesus, to refer to Himself. Four lines down, He says 'the Spirit' [Bahá'u'lláh] has come down again from heaven, "even as He came down the first time [Jesus]." We recall Bahá'u'lláh's statement: *"If ye be intent on crucifying once again Jesus, the Spirit of God, put Me to death, for He hath once more, in My person, been made manifest unto you."*
Baha'u'llah: Gleanings, 101.

We had concealed from the knowledge of the peoples of the earth and of the favoured angels hath come to pass. Say, verily, He hath testified of Me, and I do testify of Him. Indeed, He hath purposed no one other than Me. Unto this beareth witness every fair-minded and understanding soul.

"*Though beset with countless afflictions, We summon the people unto God, the Lord of names. Say, strive ye to attain that which ye have been promised in the Books of God, and walk not in the way of the ignorant. My body hath endured imprisonment that ye may be released from the bondage of self. Set your faces then towards His countenance and follow not the footsteps of every hostile oppressor. Verily, He hath consented to be sorely abased that ye may attain unto glory, and yet, ye are disporting yourselves in the vale of heedlessness. He, in truth, liveth in the most desolate of abodes for your sakes, whilst ye dwell in your palaces.*

"*Say, did ye not hearken to the Voice of the Crier,* [this refers to the Báb, the predecessor of Bahá'u'lláh] *calling aloud in the wilderness of the Bayan, bearing unto you the glad-tidings of the coming of your Lord, the All-Merciful? Lo! He is come in the sheltering shadow of Testimony, invested with conclusive proof and evidence, and those who truly believe in Him regard His presence as the embodiment of the Kingdom of God. Blessed is the man who turneth towards Him, and woe betide such as deny or doubt Him.*

"*Announce thou unto the priests: Lo! He Who is the Ruler is come. Step out from behind the veil in the name of thy Lord, He Who layeth low the necks of all men. Proclaim then unto all mankind the glad-tidings of this mighty, this glorious Revelation. Verily, He*

Who is the Spirit of Truth is come to guide you unto all truth. He speaketh not as prompted by His own self, but as bidden by Him Who is the All-Knowing, the All-Wise.

"Say, this is the One Who hath glorified the Son and hath exalted His Cause. Cast away, O peoples of the earth, that which ye have and take fast hold of that which ye are bidden by the All-Powerful, He Who is the Bearer of the Trust of God. Purge ye your ears and set your hearts towards Him that ye may hearken to the most wondrous Call which hath been raised from Sinai, the habitation of your Lord, the Most Glorious. It will, in truth, draw you nigh unto the Spot wherein ye will perceive the splendour of the light of His countenance which shineth above this luminous Horizon.

"O concourse of priests! Leave the bells, and come forth, then, from your churches. It behoveth you, in this day, to proclaim aloud the Most Great Name among the nations. Prefer ye to be silent, whilst every stone and every tree shouteth aloud: 'The Lord is come in His great glory!'? Well is it with the man who hasteneth unto Him. Verily, he is numbered among them whose names will be eternally recorded and who will be mentioned by the Concourse on High.

Thus hath it been decreed by the Spirit in this wondrous Tablet. He that summoneth men in My name is, verily, of Me, and he will show forth that which is beyond the power of all that are on earth. Follow ye the Way of the Lord and walk not in the footsteps of them that are sunk in heedlessness. Well is it with the slumberer who is stirred by the Breeze of God and ariseth from amongst the dead, directing his steps towards the Way of the Lord. Verily, such a man is regarded, in the sight of God, the True One, as a jewel amongst men and is reckoned with the blissful.

"Say: In the East the light of His Revelation hath broken; in the West have appeared the signs of His dominion. Ponder this in your hearts, O people, and be not of those who have turned a deaf ear to the admonitions of Him Who is the Almighty, the All-Praised. Let the Breeze of God awaken you. Verily, it hath wafted over the world. Well is it with him that hath discovered the fragrance thereof and been accounted among the well-assured.

"O concourse of bishops! Ye are the stars of the heaven of My knowledge. My mercy desireth not that ye should fall upon the earth. My justice, however, declareth: 'This is that which the Son hath decreed.' And whatsoever hath proceeded out of His blameless, His truth-speaking, trustworthy mouth, can never be altered. The bells, verily, peal out My Name, and lament over Me, but My spirit rejoiceth with evident gladness. The body of the Loved One yearneth for the cross, and His head is eager for the spear, in the path of the All-Merciful. The ascendancy of the oppressor can in no wise deter Him from His purpose. We have summoned all created things to attain the presence of thy Lord, the King of all names. Blessed is the man that hath set his face towards God, the Lord of the Day of Reckoning.

"O concourse of monks! If ye choose to follow Me, I will make you heirs of My Kingdom; and if ye transgress against Me, I will, in My long-suffering, endure it patiently, and I, verily, am the Ever-Forgiving, the All-Merciful.

"O land of Syria![104] *What hath become of thy righteousness? Thou art, in truth, ennobled by the footsteps of thy Lord. Hast thou perceived the fragrance of heavenly reunion, or art thou to be accounted of the heedless?*

[In the following paragraphs, Bahá'u'lláh uses 'poetic license,' employing a custom of Arabic literature, to have a city, and a mountain, speak as if with human voice. Bethlehem speaks to Bahá'u'lláh and He answers. They carry on a conversation. Mt. Sinai speaks also.]

"Bethlehem is astir with the Breeze of God. We hear her voice saying: 'O most generous Lord! Where is Thy great glory established? The sweet savours of Thy presence have quickened me, after I had melted in my separation from Thee. Praised be Thou in that Thou hast raised the veils, and come with power in evident glory.' We called unto her from behind the Tabernacle of Majesty and Grandeur: 'O Bethlehem! This Light hath risen in the orient, and travelled towards the occident, until it reached thee in the evening of its life. Tell Me then: Do the sons recognize the Father, and acknowledge Him, or do they deny Him, even as the people aforetime denied Him (Jesus)?' Whereupon she cried out saying: 'Thou art, in truth, the All-Knowing, the Best-Informed.' Verily, We behold all created things moved to bear witness unto Us. Some know Us and bear witness, while the majority bear witness, yet know Us not.

---

[104] 'Akká and Mt. Carmel, at the time of Revelation of this tablet, were in Syria. In modern times, they are in the nation of Israel.

"Mount Sinai is astir with the joy of beholding Our countenance. She hath lifted her enthralling voice in glorification of her Lord, saying: 'O Lord! I sense the fragrance of Thy garment. Methinks Thou art near, invested with the signs of God. Thou hast ennobled these regions with Thy footsteps. Great is the blessedness of Thy people, could they but know Thee and inhale Thy sweet savours; and woe betide them that are fast asleep.'

"Happy art thou who hast turned thy face towards My countenance, inasmuch as thou hast rent the veils asunder, hast shattered the idols and recognized thine eternal Lord. The people of the Qur'an [that is, Muslims] *have risen up against Us without any clear proof or evidence, tormenting Us at every moment with a fresh torment. They idly imagine that tribulations can frustrate Our Purpose. Vain indeed is that which they have imagined. Verily, thy Lord is the One Who ordaineth whatsoever He pleaseth.*

[In the following paragraphs, Bahá'u'lláh inserts a passage He had previously written to the King of Persia telling Him that He longed for crucifixion or martyrdom.]

"I never passed a tree but Mine heart addressed it saying: 'O would that thou wert cut down in My name, and My body crucified upon thee.' We revealed this passage in the Epistle to the Shah that it might serve as a warning to the followers of religions. Verily, thy Lord is the All-Knowing, the All-Wise.

"Let not the things they have perpetrated grieve thee. Truly they are even as dead, and not living. Leave them unto the dead, then turn thy face towards Him Who is the Life-Giver of the world.

Beware lest the sayings of the heedless sadden thee. Be thou steadfast in the Cause, and teach the people with consummate wisdom. Thus enjoineth thee the Ruler of earth and heaven. He is in truth the Almighty, the Most Generous. Ere long will God exalt thy remembrance and will inscribe with the Pen of Glory that which thou didst utter for the sake of His love. He is in truth the Protector of the doers of good.

"Give My remembrance to the one named Murad[105] *and say: 'Blessed art thou, O Murad, inasmuch as thou didst cast away the promptings of thine own desire and hast followed Him Who is the Desire of all mankind.'*

[The following part of Bahá'u'lláh's 'Letter to the Christians' and to you, contains what has seemed to me to be similar to Christ's Beatitudes. It is one of several similar passages in the Bahá'í Scriptures.]

"Say: Blessed the slumberer who is awakened by My Breeze. Blessed the lifeless one who is quickened through My reviving breaths. Blessed the eye that is solaced by gazing at My beauty. Blessed the wayfarer who directeth his steps towards the Tabernacle of My glory and majesty. Blessed the distressed one who seeketh refuge beneath

---

105 We do not really know to whom this letter was written, other than that the recipient was Christian. As stated earlier, we think (but do not know) that the letter may have been written to Faris Effendi, the first Christian to declare faith in Bahá'u'lláh, or, the letter may have been written in honour of him. Nor, do we know who 'Murad' is, but it sounds as if he, too, has recently declared as a follower of Bahá'u'lláh. By the way, one can find similar passages and mentions of various names of individuals in the letters of St. Paul in the New Testament.

the shadow of My canopy. Blessed the sore athirst who hasteneth to the soft-flowing waters of My loving-kindness.

"*Blessed the insatiate soul who casteth away his selfish desires for love of Me and taketh his place at the banquet table which I have sent down from the heaven of divine bounty for My chosen ones. Blessed the abased one who layeth fast hold on the cord of My glory; and the needy one who entereth beneath the shadow of the Tabernacle of My wealth. Blessed the ignorant one who seeketh the fountain of My knowledge; and the heedless one who cleaveth to the cord of My remembrance. Blessed the soul that hath been raised to life through My quickening breath and hath gained admittance into My heavenly Kingdom.*

"*Blessed the man whom the sweet savours of reunion with Me have stirred and caused to draw nigh unto the Dayspring of My Revelation. Blessed the ear that hath heard and the tongue that hath borne witness and the eye that hath seen and recognized the Lord Himself, in His great glory and majesty, invested with grandeur and dominion. Blessed are they that have attained His presence. Blessed the man who hath sought enlightenment from the Day-Star of My Word. Blessed he who hath attired his head with the diadem of My love.*

"*Blessed is he who hath heard of My grief and hath arisen to aid Me among My people. Blessed is he who hath laid down his life in My path and hath borne manifold hardships for the sake of My Name. Blessed the man who, assured of My Word, hath arisen from among the dead to celebrate My praise. Blessed is he that hath been enraptured by My wondrous melodies and hath rent the veils asunder through the potency of My might. Blessed is he who hath remained faithful to My Covenant, and whom the things of the world have not kept back from attaining My Court of holiness.*

"Blessed is the man who hath detached himself from all else but Me, hath soared in the atmosphere of My love, hath gained admittance into My Kingdom, gazed upon My realms of glory, quaffed the living waters of My bounty, hath drunk his fill from the heavenly river of My loving providence, acquainted himself with My Cause, apprehended that which I concealed within the treasury of My Words, and hath shone forth from the horizon of divine knowledge engaged in My praise and glorification. Verily, he is of Me. Upon him rest My mercy, My loving-kindness, My bounty and My glory." (Bahá'u'lláh: *Tablets of Bahá'u'lláh*, 9-19)

This is the end of Bahá'u'lláh's 'Letter to the Christians.'

[The following is from my earlier book, *Questions from Christians: About Bahá'u'lláh and the Bahá'í Faith*.]

QUESTION: I feel a sense of shock in hearing that letter. I've never read anything quite like it! It only deepens my feeling and my resolve to make a decision about Who Bahá'u'lláh is, and especially, whether or not He is the Return of Christ, as He clearly states in this letter. I do see, also, that you have not been quoting things 'out of context'. As you said, the context makes Bahá'u'lláh's statements even stronger.

RESPONSE: I can recall my own sense of 'shock' when I first read Bahá'u'lláh's 'Letter to the Christians.' It definitely calls for deep thought on the part of almost anyone who reads it. I believe a Christian cannot fail to recognize that Bahá'u'lláh is calling upon him/her to recognize Him as the Return of the Spirit of Christ and to become His disciple.

⸘

AUTHOR'S POSTSCRIPT: Though I did not think that they belonged in the body of this story, which is mostly about more distant historical figures, there are a number of persons, some of them famous Christians to me, who played a central and significant role in my own life. First and foremost, my father and mother, Rev. Lacy H. Thompson and Eva Hager Thompson. They led me to Christ. That certainly made them famous to me.

Teachers: Along the way, many teachers: Mrs. Green, Alfred Martin, Richard Martin, R. W. George, Gavin L. Doughty, Sr., Mr. Scott, Kendrick Grobel, Bard Thompson, George Noel Mayhew, Roger Shinn. Many others, of course.

Authors: My pathway to becoming a disciple of Bahá'u'lláh, as well as a disciple of Christ, was aided and encouraged by a number of authors. First, by Nels F. S. Ferre, premiere Christian theologian, who wrote *The Sun and the Umbrella*. Reading this book electrified me and made me want to go to Vanderbilt University School of Divinity (Graduate School), where he taught, for seminary training.

Then, while at Vanderbilt, I encountered a book by the famed Stanwood Cobb, a Christian who had widened his faith by declaring in the early twentieth century as a Bahá'í. Entirely by chance, (or so it would seem to others) I pulled down a book from a private library; it was entitled: *Security in a Failing World*. This was my first introduction to the Bahá'í Faith and it brought about a real thirst to learn more. Cobb has been listed earlier as a 'Famous Christian,' since he graduated from Harvard Divinity School and would have pursued the Christian ministry, until learning about the Bahá'í Faith and meeting 'Abdu'l-Bahá.

Spiritual parents: Though I regard my mother and father as spiritual parents, the spiritual parent who ushered me along into belief in Bahá'u'lláh was a man of abundant energy and boundless faith. His name was Winston Gill Evans. My next book will be a biography of Winston and his career as a Bahá'í Teacher. He is dear to me and certainly 'famous' in my own life and career and my journey of faith.

Several Bahá'ís gave me special 'parenting,' too. Among them, 'Mama' Mills, Helen McCluskey, and 'Vy,' all of Ann Arbor. In Maryland, Stanwood Cobb offered his special friendship (and became my mentor), for which I am grateful. The Bahá'ís of Nashville where I declared are outstanding to me for their work in helping me into my Declaration of Faith, among them: Georgia and Roy Miller, Maude Barnes, Mary Watkins, Casey Walton, Suzy Langford, Irma Hayden, Nellie Roche. There were others, too numerous to mention and I am fully grateful to all of them.

Special Bahá'í Friends: There are so many, but the two premier friends that must be mentioned are the two that declared at the same time as my declaration: Bill Hatcher and Lucia Graham Sims. Bahá'ís in Ann Arbor, the U. S. Virgin Islands, in Montgomery County, MD and in Baltimore are remembered. In later years, as

I have worked on several military bases, new Bahá'í friends have been discovered in Syracuse, NY, Topeka, KS and in the cities of Grand Forks, Thompson, Fargo/Moorhead, and Minot, all in North Dakota. Other new Bahá'í friends were made in Bemidji, Minnesota.

Readers of this book: My special thanks are offered to this group of friends, who responded to my request to read and criticize this book on its way to publication.

Without them, the product of this book would not be as sound and correct. Don't hold them responsible for any errors, but do credit them for whatever contribution this book makes to celebrate the history of Christian involvement in the unfolding of the Bahá'í Faith.

Needing, as I did, other assisting eyes and hands on this book project, I enlisted the service of several 'Beta' readers. Their ideas have been invaluable to me. They are:

(1) The first and very 'rough draft' version of this book was read by my daughter, Tahirih Georgine Mullen, a librarian. She swept a critical eye over the manuscript and I made many changes based on her observations, criticisms and advice. I should mention that she did not see the footnotes or the bibliography (nor did the other readers).

(2) The Rev. Barbara Berry-Bailey of the Evangelical Lutheran Church of America. She is a true servant of Christ and fortunately for me, a long-time friend and counselor. Thanks for your loving friendship and your stellar sense of humor, as well as your spiritual outlook on life. Two of her many

contribution can be seen on page 17 and in a footnote on page 115.

(3) Mrs. Marjorie Lewis. Marge is a life-long friend from college (Tarkio College) who married another friend, the Rev. John Lewis. Marge has a strong, long-term record of service to Jesus of Nazareth in many different venues. Being the wife of a minister is so much more than being a conventional 'wife.' I saw that up-close in my own mother.

In addition to her manifold duties as the 'First Lady' of a number of Churches, she had her own career as a librarian. Many thanks to you Marge. I plan to carry my friendship with you and your husband, John, into what the Qur'án calls 'the second life.' Bahá'ís are told in our scriptures that there are 'many worlds of God.' I want to be privileged to greet you in all of them.

(4) Ms. Dorothy Lemon-Thompson, my dear wife, who has now been a reader for two of my books and I will seek her wise counsel for the upcoming books that I hope to finish. May I say that my trust in her counsel is strong, particularly because she is ready to tell me when I am not being clear or not even making 'good sense.' It is really helpful to have someone who, because of their undeniable love, can be strongly critical without it seeming like an attack. Thanks, Dorothy, for all that you are to me.

Other readers were: Tom Scilley and Rod and Bobbie Scilley, servants of Bahá'u'lláh in Grand Forks, North Dakota. The input and constructive criticism of all these friends is beyond description as to its value to this project. After I thought that I would have no more readers, along came dear Minot, ND friend Jim **Knudsen**, who read the manuscript very carefully and made many valuable suggestions for improvement. **Special thanks to son Hunter** for his valued research help. I also thank anyone who looked at the text but may have been forgotten.

Special Helper: I hope that you, the reader, will understand me when I tell you that I had/have a life-long (and eternal) friend, who moved into the next life in 2012. Bahá'í Daniel Illari was a creative, thoughtful, spiritually deep person, who on the day before he died, promised me personally (upon my request) to help me from that other world, through prayer, to write this book and my recent book, *Every Good Thing*. Bahá'ís have been told by Bahá'u'lláh, that after death, they can be the prayerful 'leaven' for positive developments in this world.

Thanks Daniel, and if it's not too much to ask, please stay with me in my continued task of writing.

§

To purchase a copy of *Questions from Christians: About Bahá'u'lláh and the Bahá'í Faith*, go to amazon.com

IMPORTANT: To navigate Amazon, use the exact title of the book and the correct spelling of my name = Thom Thompson.

Hopefully, my other books are listed there too, including: *Questions From Christians: About Bahá'u'lláh and the Bahá'í Faith.* and *Every Good Thing*, my personal selection of Bahá'í Scriptures for Christian

Believers and, of course, other copies of this book, Famous *Christians: In Bahá'í History*. Soon, I hope to have *Vanderbilt Boys…and what about the Girl?* listed on Amazon. Until then, you can order it directly from me (see below). A future title will be: *Unrestrained: The Life and Work of Bahá'í Teacher Winston Gill Evans*.

<u>TO ORDER BOOKS DIRECTLY FROM THE AUTHOR</u>, use the address below.

CONNECTING WITH THE AUTHOR: Should you wish to dialogue with me about this book, to suggest a correction or an addition of a 'famous Christian' (for a future edition), please email me at: daystarthom9@yahoo.com. A second email is: daystarthom@gmail.com. Or, you can write me at: Thomas Thompson, 9911 Winands Road, Randallstown, MD 21133. I would be interested to hear from you. My cell is: 443-418-5777.

BIBLIOGRAPHY

In the search for 'Famous Christians' in Bahá'í history, the following bibliographic sources were used.

'Abdu'l-Bahá. *Paris Talks*. London: Bahá'í Publishing Trust, 1995 [1912].

'Abdu'l-Bahá. *The Promulgation of Universal Peace*. Wilmette, IL: Bahá'i Publishing. Trust, 1982.

'Abdu'l-Bahá. *A Traveler's Narrative*. Translated by Edward Granville Browne. Wilmette, IL: Bahá'i Publishing Trust, 1980.

'Abdu'l-Bahá. *Selections from the Writings of 'Abdu'l-Bahá*. Translated by Marzieh Gail. Wilmette, IL: Bahá'i Publishing Trust, 1978.

Appreciations of the Bahá'í Faith: Reprinted from The Bahá'í World, Vol. VIII. Wilmette, IL: Bahá'í Publishing Committee, 1941.

Baha'i Prayers. Wilmette, IL: Baha'i Publishing Trust, 2002 Ed.

Baha'i World. Vol. 2. Wilmette, IL: Baha'i Publishing Trust, 1928.

Baha'i World. Vol. 8. Wilmette, IL: Baha'i Publishing Trust, 1941.

Bahá'u'lláh. *Epistle to the Son of the Wolf*. Wilmette, IL: Bahá'í Publishing Trust, 1988.

Bahá'u'lláh. *Gleanings from the Writings of Bahá'u'lláh.* Compiled by Shoghi Effendi Rabbani. Wilmette, IL: Bahá'í Publishing Trust, 1976.

Bahá'u'lláh. *The Kitáb-i-Aqdas* (The Most Holy Book). Haifa:

Bahá'í World Centre, 1992.

Bahá'u'lláh. *Prayers and Meditations.* Compiled by Shoghi Effendi Rabbani. Wilmette, IL: Bahá'í Pub. Committee, 1954.

Bahá'u'lláh. *The Proclamation of Bahaullah to the Kings and Leaders of the World.* Haifa: Bahá'í World Centre, 1972.

Bahá'u'lláh. *The Summons of the Lord of Hosts: Tablets of Bahá'u'lláh.* Wilmette, IL: Bahá'í Publishing Trust, 2006.

Bahá'u'lláh. *Tablets of Bahá'u'lláh,* (Revealed after the Kitáb-i-Aqdas). Translated by Adib Taherzadeh. Wilmette, IL: Bahá'í Publishing Trust, 1988.

Balyuzi, H. M. *Bahá'u'lláh, the King of Glory.* Oxford: George Ronald, 1980.

Báb, The. *Selections from the Writings of the Báb.* Haifa: (ed. under Guidance of the Universal House of Justice), 1976.

Browne, Edward Granville. *Materials for the Study of the Bab☒i ☒religion.* Cambridge, UK: University Press, 1918.

Cedarquist, Druzelle. *The Story of Baha'u'llah: Promised One of All Religions.* Wilmette, IL: Bahá'í Publishing Trust, 2005.

Cheyne, T. K. *The Reconciliation of Races and Religions.* London: A. and C. Black, 1914.

This book is available digitally as an eBook from: www.gutenberg.org/ebooks/7995.

The Compilation of Compilations. Mona Vale, Australia: Bahá'í Publications, 2000.

Gillespie, John Birks., and Wilmot Alfred Fraser. *To Be, or Not ... to BOP.* New York City: Doubleday, 1979.

Hatcher, John. *The Ocean of His Words: A Reader's Guide to the Art of Bahá'u'lláh.* Wilmette, IL: Bahá'í Publishing. Trust, 1997.

Hofman, David. *George Townshend: Hand of the Cause of God.* (Sometime Canon of St. Patrick's Cathedral, Dublin, Archdeacon of Clonfert). Oxford: G. Ronald, 1983.

Momen, Moojan. *Bahá'u'lláh: A Short Biography.* Oxford: Oneworld, 2007.

'Nabil' (Muhammad-i-Zarandi). *The Dawnbreakers: Nabil's Narrative of the Early Days of the Bahá'í Revelation.* Translated by Shoghi Effendi Rabbani. New York: Bahá'í Publishing Trust, 1932 [1887-88].

NOTE: This book is invaluable for several reasons. First, the author interviewed many eyewitnesses to the beginnings of the Bábí and Bahá'í Faiths. He himself was a first-hand observer of many events and a devoted disciple of Bahá'u'lláh. The book was written with the assistance of Bahá'u'lláh's faithful brother, Mirzá Musa, who also was a close-in observer of both the Báb and his brother, Bahá'u'lláh. Portions of the book were reviewed by Bahá'u'lláh Himself. Other portions were reviewed by 'Abdu'l-Bahá.

Phillips, J. B. *Your God Is Too Small*. New York: Touchstone, 1997.

Pole, Wellesley Tudor. *The Silent Road: In the Light of Personal Experience*. London: Neville Spearman, 1960. This book can be accessed in PDF at bahai-library.com

Pole, Wellesley Tudor. *Writing on the Ground*. London: Neville Spearman, 1968. A portion of this book that deals with the Bahá'í Faith can be accessed in PDF at bahai-library.com

Salley, Columbus. *The Black 100: A Ranking of the Most Influential African-Americans, past and Present*. Secaucus, NJ: Carol Pub. Group, 1993.

The Seven Year Plan 1979-86: Statistical Report, Ridvan, 1983. Wilmette, IL: Bahá'í Pub. Trust, 1983.

Shoghi Effendi. *God Passes By*. Wilmette, IL: Bahá'í Publishing Trust, 1944.

Shoghi Effendi. *The Promised Day Is Come.* Wilmette, IL: Bahá'í Publishing Trust, 1961.

Star of the West.

A magazine begun in 1910 by early North American Bahá'ís (the first of its kind). It published until 1922, when superseded by World Order Magazine (see below). Stanwood Cobb (one of our 'Famous Christians') was a frequent contributor to '*Star of the West,*' and the first editor of World Order. '*Star of the West*' can be accessed on the web in several ways.

Taherzadeh, Adib. *The Revelation of Bahá'u'lláh.* Oxford: Ronald, 1977.

Published in four volumes, between 1974-77. Gives enormous detail on the Revelation of Baha'u'llah.

Thompson, Thom. *Questions from Christians: About Baha'u'llah and the Baha'i Faith.* Philadelphia, PA: Xlibris, 2001. (xlibris.com)

This book is the first in a three-part series called 'The Christian Believers Series.' It seeks to answer many common questions that Christians might have upon first encountering Bahá'u'lláh and the Bahá'í Faith. Separate chapters treat history, teachings, similarities and differences with Christianity and lists almost 100 Christian topics (such as salvation, the divinity of Christ, the Bible, life after death, etc.) with brief comment on what the Faith of Bahá'u'lláh has to say about these topics. This book and the two below can be ordered from amazon.com. Books two of this series is: *'Every Good Thing,'* which presents 'Selections from Bahá'í Scriptures Chosen for Christian Believers.' Book three of the series is this book: *Famous Christians: In Bahá'í History.*

Townshend, George. *The Mission of Bahá'u'lláh, and Other Literary Pieces.* Oxford: G. Ronald, 1952.

World Order.

A periodical published by the National Spiritual Assembly of the Bahá'ís of the United States in the early and mid-twentieth-century (and re-instated in the later years of the century) Wilmette, IL. Bahá'í Publishing Trust. One of its first editors was Stanwood Cobb (see above under 'Five Christians who Became Bahá'ís.'

Worthington, Frances. *Abraham: One God, Three Wives, Five Religions.* Wilmette, IL: Bahá'í Publishing Trust, 2011.

Made in the USA
Middletown, DE
24 January 2018